favourites

100 deliciously easy recipes from Asda customers

RECIPES TESTED BY THE ASDA CHEFS

favourites

Asda Stores Ltd

Southbank, Great Wilson Street, Leeds LS11 5AD

www.asda.com

ISBN: 1-903901-22-7

Printed by Scotprint. Colour reproduction by Graphic Facilities

Published for Asda by Publicis Blueprint, 82 Baker Street, London W1U 6TG.

Editor Liz Trigg

Food Consultant Alasdair McWhirter

Photography Joff Lee, Terry Benson, Rob Whitrow

Home Economist Kathryn Hawkins, assisted by Jayne Cross

Styling Maria Kelly

Art Director Louise Rickard

Managing Editor Ward Hellewell

Account Manager Victoria Leather

Publishing Account Director Geri Richards

contents

using the recipes

● All spoon measurements are level. Tablespoons are assumed to be 15ml. Metric and imperial weights are given, except for food sold in standard sized packaging, such as cans. Conversions are not always exact, so use either metric or imperial throughout each recipe, where possible.

● Unless otherwise stated, eggs and individual fruit and vegetables are all assumed to be medium sized.

● If using unpeeled fruit or vegetables, wash them thoroughly beforehand.

● Recipes using raw or partially-cooked eggs should be avoided by infants, the elderly, pregnant women, anyone suffering or recovering from an illness.

● Check labels of commercially prepared ingredients if you suffer from nut, milk or gluten intolerance. Milk and gluten free statements on recipes are based on the use of Asda brand ingredients, where they exist.

● Timings and the number of servings given are a guide only. Preparation times may vary according to techniques used and cooking times may vary with the type of oven used.

● Some ingredients may not be available in all Asda stores.

● All recipes have been tested and edited where appropriate.

introduction

We at Asda are always interested in learning more about what our customers like and want, and last year, we hit upon a unique way of finding out what they love to cook and eat. We launched a nationwide competition asking people to send in their favourite recipes and the response was amazing. Recipes poured in from busy mums, glamorous grannies, single men and hundreds of other people, from all walks of life and every corner of the country. This book includes the pick of them – the 100 most successful recipes.

When it came to choosing the winning recipes, the book's editor Liz Trigg had the help of Asda's two innovation chefs, Neil Nugent and Jonathan Moore. They were looking for dishes that were simple to make, reliable and totally delicious! And they also took care to ensure the winning dishes offered great value, using ingredients available at Asda's low prices – always.

Throughout the book, Neil and Jonathan reveal some invaluable tips, shortcuts and secrets and have provided loads of great ideas on how to vary some of the dishes. They have also passed on some of the recipes they like to cook at home for their own families.

Favourites is not just about food – it's also a book about people and today's busy lifestyle. Each chapter has been designed to fit in with a particular need or occasion – whether it's feeding a hungry family or laying on a special girls' night in. Whatever demands there are on your life at the moment, I hope you'll find plenty of recipes that suit you perfectly!

Tony

Tony DeNunzio, Chief Operating Officer, Asda

 **Liz Trigg** has been food editor on top magazines, run her own catering company, written cookbooks and appeared as a chef on TV. She is currently principal of the Asda Academy of Food Skills.

 **Neil Nugent** has been a chef for 19 years and has worked in restaurants around the world, including France and the Caribbean. He joined Asda four years ago and is now an innovation chef.

 **Jonathan Moore** is a classically trained chef who has worked in top restaurants, including a five-star country hotel in Devon. He joined Asda four years ago, and is now an innovation chef.

no time to cook

Whether you've been rushing home from work, or coping with a house full of children, being expected to get a meal on the table in seconds flat is never easy. The recipes in this chapter have been chosen because they are quick to prepare, satisfying and are great value. Better still, they use simple ingredients that you are likely to have in your fridge or cupboard, so hopefully it won't matter if you haven't had time to get to the shops.

spanish omelette

If you have some leftover cooked potatoes, this omelette is a great way to use them up. It tastes terrific hot or cold – try making a lunchtime sandwich of it with fresh bread, lots of lettuce and some mayo

 Preparing: 5 mins

 Cooking: 25 mins

 Serves 1

 Milk and gluten free

Ingredients

200g/7oz or 2 small potatoes, diced

1tbsp olive oil

1 small onion, sliced

3 eggs, lightly beaten

Ketchup or mayonnaise, to serve

Salt and freshly ground black pepper

1 Boil the potatoes for 5-10 minutes, until just soft.

2 Meanwhile, in a small frying pan, heat the olive oil and fry the onion over a low heat until it is just starting to go brown – this will take about 15-20 minutes. Drain the potatoes and add them to the pan with the onion.

3 Season the eggs well and pour them over the potato and onion mixture. Stir the mixture once and leave to cook through – this should take about 5-10 minutes. When it's done, flip the omelette onto a plate and serve with ketchup or mayonnaise.

Robert Clark
London

Cooking and eating are two of my most favourite things – I can never understand why some people aren't interested in food! A lot of people seem to worry about things not turning out perfectly and looking like they do on telly or in a magazine, but I think that's part of the fun of cooking. I'm not that fussed about presentation – as long as it tastes good, that's the main thing. This is one of those recipes you can make when you want something really quick and easy – I've always got eggs, potatoes and onions in the house, so it's one of my reliable stand-by dishes. It's vegetarian, too, so everyone can enjoy it.

the asda chefs say...
If you are not too worried about a few extra calories, deep-fry the potato until brown – this will speed up the potato cooking time and make it tastier.

quick beef bolognese

 Preparing: 10 mins

 Cooking: 45 mins

 Serves 4

 Sauce freezes well

There's something really comforting about a homemade spaghetti Bolognese, especially when it only takes 10 minutes to prepare. The pasta makes the meat go a long way, so it's very good value, too

Ingredients

455g/1lb minced beef

1 large onion, finely chopped

115g/4oz button mushrooms, finely chopped

1 garlic clove, chopped

70g can of tomato purée

1 beef stock cube

15g pack of fresh basil, roughly chopped (optional)

285g/10oz spaghetti

55g/2oz Parmesan cheese, grated or shaved

1 Heat a large frying pan and brown the mince, draining off any excess fat. Add the onion, mushrooms, garlic and tomato purée and cook for a further minute or two.

2 Crumble the stock cube into 175ml/6floz boiling water and add to the beef mixture. Simmer for 30 minutes, then stir in the basil, if using.

3 Cook the spaghetti according to the pack instructions and serve with the Bolognese sauce and Parmesan cheese.

the asda chefs say...

Add some chopped bacon with the onions and a dash of Worcestershire sauce to give the Bolognese sauce a bit of spice. If you prefer a thicker sauce, add a tin of chopped plum tomatoes and use slightly less water with the stock cube.

Lynn Tibbott
Asda Colleague, Cwmbran

I have a very fussy family. None of them like sauces from a packet or a jar, some of them don't like garlic and I myself am not keen on lots of spices. So I have to be very adaptable in the kitchen! I do all my cooking from scratch, so my recipes need to be very simple and this beef Bolognese is a quick and easy family favourite. I really admire celebrity chefs who can use a simple ingredient to give a new twist to a well-known meal. I love watching Brian Turner on *Ready Steady Cook* for his ideas, like adding beer to a batter mix to totally transform a plate of fish and chips.

leek, cheese and bacon omelette

A really quick dish made from ingredients you'll probably have in the fridge. It's all made in one pan, so you will also save time when it comes to doing the washing up

 Preparing: 10 mins

 Cooking: 15 mins

 Serves 2

 Gluten free

Ingredients

3tbsp olive or vegetable oil

4 rashers back bacon

30g/1oz butter

2tbsp white wine vinegar

2 leeks, trimmed and thinly sliced

5 eggs, lightly beaten

2tbsp fresh parsley, chopped

75g/3oz Cheddar cheese, grated

A pinch of ground nutmeg

Salt and freshly ground black pepper

1 Heat 1tbsp oil and fry the bacon in a medium-sized non-stick frying pan over a medium heat for 2 minutes on each side. Remove from the pan.

2 Add half the butter, 1tbsp oil, the vinegar and leeks to the pan and cook for 5 minutes, until the leeks brown. Remove from the pan and wipe it clean.

3 Heat the remaining oil and butter in the pan over a gentle heat. Season the eggs and add to the pan. Cook for 2-3 minutes, stirring until half the egg has set. Then add the bacon, the leeks, half the parsley, the cheese and the nutmeg. Cook for another minute. Fold the omelette over, garnish with the rest of the parsley and serve immediately.

the asda chefs say...

To make this suitable for a vegetarian, leave out the bacon and add some chopped walnuts instead.

Liam Mullins
Leeds, West Yorkshire

I'm a self-taught cook and I get a lot of my ideas from eating out at restaurants and other people's houses. If I've had something really delicious, I'll usually try to recreate it at home. The best bit about cooking for me is the eating bit! One of the first things I ever cooked was spaghetti Bolognese – I'm ashamed to say that once when I made it I was so eager to get to the table I ended up spilling the whole lot down the dining room wall. These days I do a pretty mean Thai curry; but if I'm eating out I can't resist Chinese.

tasty tortellini

When you're in a hurry but still want something substantial, this fresh pasta dish is the answer. The mushroom soup makes an instant sauce and the whole dish is bursting with flavour

 Preparing: 5 mins

 Cooking: 20 mins

 Serves 4

 Quick but filling

Ingredients

1tbsp olive oil

1 onion, thinly sliced

8 rashers unsmoked rindless bacon, cut into strips

1tsp lazy ginger

1tsp lazy garlic

295g can of condensed mushroom soup

300g/10½oz fresh tortellini

55g/2oz Cheddar cheese, grated (optional)

Chopped parsley, to garnish

Freshly ground black pepper

1 Heat the oil in a frying pan and gently fry the onion for 5 minutes. Add the bacon and cook for a further 5 minutes until it's almost cooked. Then add the ginger and garlic and fry for a further 2-3 minutes.

2 Add the soup and 115ml/4fl oz water and mix thoroughly. Bring to the boil and simmer for 5 minutes, then season. Towards the end of the cooking time, cook the tortellini according to the pack instructions in a large pan of boiling water.

3 Drain the pasta and serve immediately, pouring the sauce over and sprinkling with the cheese, if using, and parsley. Serve with your favourite steamed vegetables – try baby sweetcorn, broccoli or mange tout.

the asda chefs say...

As an alternative to the mushroom soup and water, why not try adding half a tub of Asda Fresh pesto?

Hitesh Mistry
Bolton, Lancashire

I do most of the cooking during the week as I get home from work earlier than my wife, so by the time she walks in the door, her dinner is on the table. We both love food and our lives revolve around our meals – to the extent that as soon as we've finished one dinner, we begin to plan what we're going to eat the night after! We're quite adventurous and like to try different dishes at local restaurants as well as on holiday. The only time we've been put off a meal was when we ordered a seafood paella and there were a few too many octopus tentacles in it!

easy pasta

Everyone loves pasta and if you use fresh ingredients, even the simplest dish, like this one from Asda chef Neil Nugent, will taste fantastic. The soft poached egg enriches the pasta, making it even more delicious

 Preparing: 5 mins

 Cooking: 15 mins

 Serves 4

 Milk free

Ingredients

400g/14oz Quick Cook pasta farfalle or penne

2tbsp extra virgin olive oil

115g/4oz pancetta

1 garlic clove, finely sliced

255g/9oz cherry tomatoes, halved

4 eggs

15g pack of fresh basil or parsley, roughly chopped

Freshly ground black pepper

1 Bring a large pan of water to the boil and cook the pasta according to the pack instructions.

2 While the pasta is cooking, heat the oil in a frying pan and cook the pancetta and garlic for 1 minute. Add the tomatoes and cook for a few more minutes.

3 Meanwhile, poach the eggs, one at a time, in a separate pan of boiling water – stir the water with a spoon to make it swirl before you add the egg so the white clings together. The eggs only take 2-3 minutes as the yolks should still be runny.

4 Drain the pasta, add it to the tomato mixture and stir well. Add the herbs, season with pepper and divide into 4 bowls. Top each with a poached egg and serve.

cooking pasta

Neil recommends using about 100g/3½oz of pasta per person for a filling main course. His top pasta tip? Use the biggest pan you have and plenty of boiling water – 1 litre per 100g of pasta. You don't really need to add salt or oil to the water as this will affect the flavour of the pasta.

chef's secrets...
Neil Nugent
Asda innovation chef

It's best to cook the sauce in a wok as it makes it easy to mix everything together well. You won't need any extra salt – the pancetta is salty enough to season the dish. The egg should be mixed into the pasta to coat and enrich it.

turkey satay stir-fry

A healthy recipe using lots of store cupboard ingredients that's fresh, crunchy and very tasty – and it looks great, too. To make it even easier, buy a ready-prepared stir-fry veg mix, then you can prepare it in no time

 Preparing: 10 mins

 Cooking: 15 mins

 Serves 4

 Milk free

Ingredients

250g/9oz thick dried noodles

4tbsp smooth peanut butter

1tbsp tomato purée

2tsp Dijon mustard

1tbsp balsamic vinegar

Juice of 1 lime

2tbsp sunflower oil

650g/1lb 7oz turkey breasts, cut into 5cm/2in strips

140g/5oz green beans, halved

1 red pepper, de-seeded and cut into 2.5cm/1in strips

4 spring onions, chopped

2 garlic cloves, finely chopped

15g pack of fresh coriander, chopped

Salt and freshly ground black pepper

1 Cook the noodles according to the pack instructions. Meanwhile make the peanut sauce. Stir together the peanut butter, tomato purée, mustard, vinegar, seasoning and lime juice with 4tbsp of water.

2 Heat the oil in a wok or large frying pan over a high heat until it starts smoking. Add the turkey, beans and pepper and stir-fry for 4 minutes. Then add the spring onions and garlic and stir-fry for a further 3 minutes.

3 Pour over the peanut sauce and stir in the noodles. Heat through for another 3 minutes until the sauce is bubbling, then stir in the coriander and serve immediately.

the asda chefs say...

You can use all sorts of different vegetables (cut into even-sized pieces) for this recipe – try broccoli, carrots, courgettes or cabbage. You can also use chicken, pork or beef instead of turkey.

Pauline Harrison

Asda Colleague, Bouldon

I'm a collector of recipes – I've got big files of them that I've cut out of magazines and newspapers, cookery cards – all kinds of things. I also love TV cookery shows and my ambition is to go on *Ready Steady Cook*. I'm events co-ordinator at Asda but I used to work on the checkout and it really opens your mind as to what other people eat. I used to be really nosey and if I saw an unusual ingredient in someone's shopping I'd ask them what they were going to do with it. I got quite a few good ideas that way!

speedy burgers

These burgers can be made in minutes. The kids will love them and you know what they contain

 Preparing: 10 mins

 Cooking: 20 mins

 Serves 4

 Great for kids

Ingredients

40g packet of French onion soup

455g/1lb minced pork

1 egg

1 onion, chopped

4 white baps

2 tomatoes, sliced

200g bag of mixed salad leaves

Ketchup, sweetcorn relish or mustard

Salt and freshly ground black pepper

1 Preheat the grill to medium. Mix the first 4 ingredients together, season and shape into 4 burgers.

2 Grill the burgers for 10 minutes on each side, making sure they are cooked right through.

3 Serve on a fresh white bap with tomato slices, salad leaves and ketchup, relish or mustard.

Jane Jones
Fareham, Hampshire

My three boys are all sports mad and they have hollow legs, so I'm always trying to make things that are filling, as well as nutritious and tasty. I came up with these burgers a few years ago and I think the pork works really well. The boys love them and they're a lot nicer than frozen ones. A friend suggested I season them with the soup mix – I am sure you could use any flavour.

the asda chefs say...

You can also use lean beef mince for this recipe and add the kids' favourite flavouring, such as barbecue or brown sauce, to the meat mixture.

Preparing: 5 mins

 Cooking: 2 mins

 Serves 1

 Vegetarian dish

banana on toast

Speed is the key with this instant hunger buster, it's quick enough to make during the commercial break!

Ingredients

2 slices of bread – use a French stick, ciabatta or crusty round loaf

2tbsp peanut butter – you might need a little more, depending on the size of the bread slices

1 large banana, sliced diagonally in 1cm/½in pieces

1 Preheat the grill until hot and toast the bread lightly on one side only.

2 Spread the untoasted sides with peanut butter and grill again for a minute or so.

3 Arrange the sliced banana on the toast and serve.

the asda chefs say...

Believe it or not, crispy bacon or sliced apple both work really well as a change to the banana.

Christian McCandless
Asda Colleague, Stafford

I love cooking, but I wouldn't claim to be an expert in the kitchen. I cook most nights and usually end up making something like lasagne or a chilli con carne, but sometimes I just want something that's really quick and simple. This recipe is one of my favourite snacks – once the grill is hot, you really can make the whole thing during the TV ads.

pizza baps

These mini pizzas cost next to nothing to make – just mix and match the toppings to suit your mood!

 Preparing: 10 mins

 Cooking: 10 mins

 Serves 4

 Scrummy finger food

Ingredients

4 white, or wholemeal, baps

1 garlic clove, crushed

55g/2oz butter

1tsp dried mixed herbs

2 large beef tomatoes, sliced thinly

125g/4½oz mozzarella or Cheddar cheese, grated

50g tin of anchovy fillets

12 black olives, pitted and halved

15g pack of fresh basil, roughly chopped (optional)

Freshly ground black pepper

1 Preheat the grill. Cut the baps in half, horizontally, and put them cut side down on a baking tray. Toast for about 2 minutes until golden. Mix the garlic with the butter, herbs and black pepper. Spread the mixture evenly on the untoasted side of each bap.

2 Cover the baps with slices of tomato and grill for a further 3 minutes. Top with the cheese and grill for another 2-3 minutes, until it's melted. Garnish with the anchovies, olives and basil. Serve immediately.

Tim Wickenden
Asda Colleague, Canterbury

I cook everyday and pay special attention to making sure that the dishes are nutritious and full of vitamins. It's not just something I do out of necessity – it's an activity I genuinely enjoy. If there's a family party going on, I'll do it all; organising, catering – I love to cook. My family are more than happy to see me in the kitchen and we enjoy a varied and healthy diet.

tomatoes on toast

 Preparing: 5 mins

 Cooking: 10 mins

 Serves 1

 Made in one pan

Ingredients

2 rashers streaky bacon

30g/1oz butter

3 tomatoes, cut in half

1tsp caster sugar (optional)

2 thick slices white bread

2tbsp double cream

Salt and freshly ground black pepper

1 Heat a non-stick frying pan and cook the bacon until crispy. Drain on kitchen paper while you cook the tomatoes.

2 Melt the butter and fry the tomatoes cut side down until they are soft. Sprinkle on the sugar, if using, to help them caramelise. When they are nearly done, toast the bread.

3 Add the cream to the tomatoes and heat until bubbling. Season, then pour the whole lot over the toast. Serve with the bacon on top.

the asda chefs say...

Stir ½tsp French mustard into the cream.

Use any tomatoes in your fridge that are a bit over-ripe to make this totally irresistible snack

Valerie Sprague
Asda Colleague, Hull Hessle Rd

I hate slaving over a hot stove and I try to be in and out of the kitchen in less than 30 minutes when I'm cooking. It's an invigorating and enjoyable way to make meals in minutes and doesn't sacrifice any of the taste. This recipe, uses one pan, takes only 15 minutes start to finish, and is absolutely delicious. It's the perfect snack to have in front of the TV.

grilled brie and cranberry toasts

Brie and cranberries are a match made in heaven and this is a meltingly delicious way to combine them. Serve it with a side salad for a well-balanced meal

Ingredients

1 medium French stick, sliced diagonally into 12 slices

6tbsp cranberry sauce

285g/10oz Brie cheese, cut into large thin slices

Freshly ground black pepper

1 Preheat the grill. Put the bread on kitchen foil and toast on each side for 1-2 minutes or until golden.

2 Spread ½tbsp of the cranberry sauce on each toast and cover with the slices of Brie. Take care to cover all the bread to stop it burning. Season with pepper and grill again for about 3 minutes, until the cheese is melted and slightly golden. Serve immediately.

Ruth Drury
Leeds, West Yorkshire

I learned to cook from my mum when I was young and, over the years, I've developed a few specialities that I can always rely on. My veggie enchiladas always go down well with guests. I love eating out as well, nothing too fancy – I'm probably happiest with a really nice veggie pizza! I get a lot of ideas from books and magazines and I'm willing to try almost anything, so it's not unusual for there to be the odd kitchen catastrophe. Once I was melting chocolate in a microwave and ended up burning it – the whole kitchen filled with smoke!

the asda chefs say...

This also works well with other fruity preserves – the sweet, fruity flavour goes very well with the creamy, melting Brie cheese. Try using plum conserve or redcurrant jelly.

savoury cabbage

Using your microwave to cook vegetables saves time and it cooks cabbage beautifully. Always let the cabbage stand to help its flavours develop and cool slightly. This is delicious served with chicken, pork or game

Preparing: 5 mins

Cooking: 5 mins

Serves 4

Milk and gluten free

Ingredients

Half a white or red cabbage, shredded

1 onion, chopped

1tsp sesame oil

55g/2oz raisins

Salt and freshly ground black pepper

1 Put all the ingredients into a large microwavable bowl and mix well so all the cabbage is coated in the oil and seasoning.

2 Microwave on HIGH for 5 minutes, stirring twice during cooking.

3 Leave to stand for a minute then drain any excess liquid off before serving.

Isobel Connell
Meols, Merseyside

I cook most evenings, and usually I quite enjoy it. But when I get the opportunity I certainly appreciate the occasional break. The trouble is that if someone else in the family cooks I still end up having to clear it up, so I prefer to go out to a restaurant! When I've got time, I quite like watching celebrity chefs on telly but I don't think many of them have got much idea of what it's really like working full-time, managing a family and having to get a meal on the table most nights!

the asda chefs say...

Try adding a peeled and chopped Bramley apple. If you don't have a microwave, cook the cabbage in a covered saucepan over a gentle heat for about 15 minutes or until soft.

a night in with the telly

Few things are more relaxing than putting your feet up in front of the telly with a plateful of your favourite food. To make sure you don't miss an exciting twist in your favourite drama, or a vital clue in a whodunit, the recipes in this chapter are either very quick to make or can be prepared in advance. They include exciting ways of combining fresh ingredients and there are a couple of snacks that are so simple, you can throw them together during a commercial break.

garlic bread italiano

Settle down for a night on the sofa with this quick and easy way to combat the mid-evening munchies

 Preparing: 5 mins

 Cooking: 10 mins

 Serves 4

 Vegetarian dish

Ingredients

125g/4½oz butter

2 garlic cloves, crushed

2tbsp dried mixed herbs

1 French stick cut into 10cm/4in lengths, then in half

2 x 125g/4½oz buffalo mozzarella cheeses, sliced thickly

Freshly ground black pepper

A few sundried tomatoes, to garnish

1 Preheat the grill. Melt the butter in a pan and gently fry the garlic for 2-3 minutes. Sieve the mixture and discard the garlic pulp. Add the herbs and season with black pepper.

2 Toast the bread lightly under the grill. Drizzle the garlic butter onto the toast and top with a slice of mozzarella.

3 Put under the grill until the mozzarella starts to melt. Garnish with the sundried tomatoes.

the asda chefs say...

If you like your bread really garlicky, use 4 cloves of garlic.

Michelle Read
Eastry, Kent

This recipe is ideal for family gatherings and I first tried it when my parents were having a party. It takes no more than 10 minutes and everyone seems to like it.

I get a lot of pleasure from cooking and spend quite a bit of time tinkering around in the kitchen. I try to eat as healthily as possible, but I also have a sweet tooth and love to experiment – especially when it comes to making desserts.

Preparing: 5 mins

 Cooking: 20 mins

 Serves 3

 Scrummy finger food

Ingredients

1 large onion, sliced

55g/2oz butter

1tbsp vegetable oil

6 finger rolls

210g can of 12 mini hot dogs

3tbsp sweet chilli sauce, mustard or tomato ketchup

1 Preheat the oven to 190C/375F/ Gas 5.

2 Gently fry the onion in the butter and oil until soft and golden, this takes about 15 minutes. Split the finger rolls and fill with the onion and two mini hot dogs. Place on a baking sheet, and bake for 4 minutes until piping hot.

3 Spoon over the chilli sauce, mustard or ketchup and serve.

the asda chefs say...

Prepare these up to 3 hours in advance, then pop them in the oven when you're ready to serve. Replace the hot dogs with mini burgers made from the speedy burgers recipe (see page 20), making 6 mini burgers instead of 4 large ones.

mini hot dogs

These spicy little hot dogs are ideal finger food and the perfect snack to go with your favourite movie

Helen Pattison

Asda Colleague, Peterlee

I like to be in and out of the kitchen as quickly as possible and this recipe allows me to do just that. Whether you're catering for a horde of ravenous children at a party or looking for something quick and easy to eat in the garden, this recipe is a winner – no plates, no washing up! You can add whatever sauce or relish you like to make them a little bit different.

mexican tortilla

If you like a little spice in your life, here's a simple and easy snack from Neil Nugent that can be made in minutes. Best of all, you can eat these tortillas with your fingers so there's less washing up to do!

 Preparing: 5 mins

 Cooking: 10 mins

 Serves 4

 Spicy snack

Ingredients

1 red onion, roughly chopped

6 vine tomatoes, roughly chopped

1 garlic clove, crushed

Juice of 1 lime

1 red chilli, de-seeded and finely chopped

15g pack of fresh coriander, chopped

Pack of 8 tortillas

200g/7oz Monterey Jack cheese or mature Cheddar cheese, grated

40g bag of fresh rocket, to serve

Freshly ground black pepper

1 Preheat the oven to 200C/400F/Gas 6.

2 Make the salsa by mixing the onion, tomatoes, garlic, lime juice, chilli and coriander together. Drain the salsa reserving the juice.

3 Place the tortillas on a baking sheet, spoon on the salsa and top with the cheese. Place in the oven and bake for 8-10 minutes.

4 Spoon over the salsa juice, season with black pepper and serve with fresh rocket or salad leaves.

chef's secret...
Neil Nugent
Asda innovation chef

For a quicker version, use a ready-made salsa. Lemons or oranges work just as well as limes in this recipe.

Nice 'n' spicy

You may have to experiment a bit to get the spiciness of this dish just right for your taste. There is actually a measurement, called the Scoville scale, for gauging how hot chillies are, but in general, the larger the chilli, the milder the flavour. When you are preparing your chillies, make sure that you wash your hands well with soap immediately afterwards – otherwise any juice left on your fingers could get into your eyes and be extremely painful.

quick tapas

Here are three tasty treats that will add a little Spanish spice to any evening – whether you're on your own or entertaining, you're likely to develop a Latin passion for these moreish little morsels

 Preparing: 10 mins

 No cooking required

 Serves 4

 Great for parties, too

Ingredients

Peppers and chorizo

80g pack of sliced chorizo

1 red pepper, deseeded and cut into squares

Pan con tomate – tomato bread with Serrano ham

1 French stick or ciabatta, sliced

1 large garlic clove, halved

3 ripe tomatoes, halved

2tbsp extra virgin olive oil

2 x 60g packs of sliced Serrano ham

Freshly ground black pepper

Stuffed olives

1 jar of olives stuffed with red peppers or anchovies

1 Fold the chorizo slices into quarters to make triangles. Thread alternate pieces of red pepper and chorizo onto cocktail sticks.

2 Toast the bread, and as soon as it comes out of the toaster, rub the garlic over it, then crush a halved tomato over each slice, discarding the leftover skins. Drizzle the bread with olive oil and top with a slice of Serrano ham and a grinding of pepper.

3 Put the olives in a small bowl.

the asda chefs say...

Use any colour pepper with the chorizo. Try to use Spanish ingredients, wherever possible, such as spicy chorizo sausage and Serrano ham. However, if you wish, you can use Parma ham instead of Serrano ham as it is cured in the same way.

Kate Drury
Oxford, Oxfordshire

I am a student, reading French and Spanish. I spent a year in South America, and also spent some time working as an au pair in Spain, which is where I learned how to make lots of tapas dishes. I guess that's where I get my love of Spanish-style food from. My idea of heaven is a rich Spanish wine and lovely tapas. I really like the simplicity of them – they're so easy to do but you still get lots of different flavours. I also like baking cakes and sweet things – which I learned to do from watching my grandma.

nifty nachos

A great idea for a last-minute TV snack – you can make these Mexican-style nachos as spicy as you like

 Preparing: 5 mins

 Cooking: 5 mins

 Serves 2-3

 Vegetarian dish

Ingredients

200g bag of plain tortillas

300g jar of salsa

2 red chillies, de-seeded and finely chopped

225g/8oz Monterey Jack or mature Cheddar cheese, grated

142ml pot of sour cream

1 Preheat the grill. On a large, shallow ovenproof dish, spread the tortillas out in a layer, top with the salsa and red chillies and sprinkle over the cheese.

2 Heat under the grill until the cheese is melted and golden. Serve with sour cream.

Carl Walker
Asda Colleague, Pudsey

I've been cooking since I was knee high to a grasshopper! I like to eat at Chinese restaurants, but there's nothing like home cooking, and I make lots of stir fries and rice dishes myself. This year I visited New York, and I have to say it is my favourite place for food. All those huge steaks! My partner and I both like to make up new dishes, and we often play *Ready Steady Cook* together at home!

the asda chefs say...
You can add your own toppings after grilling – try finely chopped red and green peppers or spring onions, or cubed avocado and coriander leaves.

Preparing: 10 mins

 Cooking: 45 mins

 Serves 6

 Gluten free

baked cheeses

This dish is a bit like a soufflé and a bit like a quiche, but it's much easier and quicker to prepare

Ingredients

2tsp butter, melted

455g/1lb tub of natural cottage cheese, strained

455g/1lb red Leicester cheese, grated

3 eggs, beaten

1 red pepper, de-seeded and chopped

Half a bunch of spring onions, chopped

3 beefsteak tomatoes

1tsp caster sugar

1 Preheat the oven to 180C/350F/ Gas 4. Grease a 23cm/9in ovenproof dish with the butter.

2 Mix the cottage cheese, red Leicester, eggs, red pepper and spring onions together. Pour into the dish and bake for 45 minutes until risen and brown.

3 Meanwhile, cut the tomatoes in half, sprinkle with caster sugar and cook in an ovenproof dish at the same time as the cheese.

4 Let the baked cheeses rest for 5 minutes, then serve on the cooked tomatoes.

Patrina Law
Wheatley, Oxford

I've been a vegetarian for 20 years. I love vegetarian food because it's so colourful and exciting – and healthy, too. This is one of my mum's ideas – when I left home I took a lot of her recipes with me! She always tells me that when you make a meal for somebody else it's an act of love and that's why I enjoy cooking for my friends – it's a way of saying you care about them.

tikka risotto

This mouthwatering blend of Indian and Italian cuisine is a simple solution to rumbling tums. A doddle to prepare, and very inexpensive to make, it's a sure-fire winner for family evenings in

 Preparing: 2 mins

 Cooking: 30 mins

 Serves 4

 Quick and easy

Ingredients

2 x 120g packets of Smart Price golden vegetable rice

300g/10½oz fresh mixed vegetables, such as carrots, broccoli, cauliflower and fresh peas

Half a 500g jar of Good for you! 25% less fat chicken tikka sauce

Juice of 1 lemon

15g pack of fresh coriander, roughly chopped

1 Pour the rice into a medium-sized saucepan, and cook according to the pack instructions.

2 Once the rice is boiling, add the carrots and cook for 5 minutes. Then add the broccoli, cauliflower and peas, and simmer on a low heat until all the water has evaporated and the rice is cooked.

3 Add the sauce and mix it in well. Just before serving stir in the lemon juice and coriander and gently heat the mixture to make a spicy risotto.

Miss C Nigam
New Southgate, London

This is so simple to prepare and it's something you can just throw together at the last minute using whatever frozen vegetables you have in the freezer. Just make sure you keep a jar of the sauce and a packet of the rice in the cupboard at all times! It's tasty, easy to make and healthy. The idea of a tikka risotto might seem strange to some people but if you think about it, it's just like a vegetable curry and rice, all in one dish.

the asda chefs say...
You can add chunks of cooked chicken breast when you pour in the sauce. Try other ready-made curry sauces.

mozzarella, avocado and pesto salad

Savour the flavours of Italy with this heavenly salad that will really get your tastebuds tingling. Quick enough to make as a snack, light enough for an evening meal

 Preparing: 15 mins

 Cooking: 2 mins

 Serves 2

 Gluten free

Ingredients

1 garlic clove, crushed

15g pack of fresh growing basil

30g/1oz Parmesan cheese, freshly grated

85g/3oz pine nuts, toasted

4tbsp extra virgin olive oil

Juice of half a lemon

125g/4½oz mozzarella cheese, cut into rough chunks

1 ripe avocado, peeled and roughly chopped

1 pack of green mixed salad leaves

Freshly ground black pepper

1 Put the garlic, basil, Parmesan cheese and 55g/2oz of the pine nuts in a liquidiser and process until you have a thick paste. Add the olive oil and lemon juice with the blades still running. Pour the mixture into the base of a large salad bowl.

2 Add the mozzarella cheese and avocado, and toss well. Gently stir in the leaves and season with pepper. Dry-fry the remaining pine nuts in a non-stick frying pan for a couple of minutes until lightly toasted, then sprinkle them over the salad and serve immediately.

the asda chefs say...

Try splashing a little balsamic vinegar over this salad, or toast some ciabatta bread and spoon the salad on top for a delicious open sandwich. Sprinkling lemon juice over the chopped avocado will stop it discolouring.

Nick Shorthose
Leeds, West Yorkshire

My proudest cookery moment (apart from appearing in this book, of course), was when I won a recipe competition in a Sunday newspaper and ended up appearing on the same page as Gary Rhodes. My biggest love is pasta and curry dishes – the great thing about them is that you can add whatever you like and you can't really go wrong. Having said that, I have had one or two mishaps in the kitchen, including nearly burning the whole place down one Christmas while trying to light the gas cooker!

west african curry

What would Friday evening be without a curry? There's no need to call the local takeaway – this dish is a little bit sweet, more than a little bit spicy and sure to satisfy your appetite

 Preparing: 10 mins

 Cooking: 35 mins

 Serves 4

 Milk and gluten free

Ingredients

2tbsp olive oil

1 onion, finely chopped

2 garlic cloves, finely chopped

3 whole cloves

1tbsp garam masala

1tsp ground turmeric

2tsp ground cumin

1tsp chilli powder

2tsp ground coriander

1tbsp dried mixed herbs

455g/1lb minced lamb

55g/2oz flaked almonds, plus extra toasted flaked almonds, to garnish

2tbsp mango chutney or Branston pickle

55g/2oz sultanas

1tbsp tomato purée

115g/4oz frozen peas

2 medium tomatoes, diced, to garnish

1 In a large wok or frying pan, heat the olive oil and gently fry the onions until softened, but not coloured – this takes about 10-15 minutes. Add the garlic, spices and herbs, and sauté for a further 1-2 minutes.

2 Add the mince and fry until well browned, then stir in the almonds, chutney or pickle, sultanas and tomato purée. Cook, stirring well, for about 15 minutes. If the mince appears too dry, add 100ml/3½fl oz of water. Add the peas to the pan 5 minutes before serving. Garnish with the tomatoes and toasted flaked almonds and serve with naan bread or rice.

the asda chefs say...

To spare yourself the chore of chopping the garlic and onion, use a food processor – you can halve the preparation time. If you like your curries a little less spicy, reduce the amount of cumin and chilli powder slightly.

Mrs D Shepherd
Broughton Astley, Leicestershire

When my husband and I were first married we used to visit a pub at Church Lawford in Warwickshire. Our treat was this 'West African' curry – a recipe that the owner of the pub had come across when he was serving in the armed forces. He used to make it in different grades of heat and would never divulge the recipe, so I had to try to recreate it. It took me about 20 attempts before I arrived at this version, but it's still not the same as the original. I've given up trying to get it exactly the same – now I vary it, depending on what I've got in the fridge or what's on special offer!

sweetcorn fritters

Share these yummy fritters with all the family – eat them with your fingers and they taste even better!

 Preparing: 10 mins

 Cooking: 12 mins

 Makes 12 fritters

 Great for kids

Ingredients

2tbsp milk

3tbsp Greek yogurt

2 eggs

80g/2¾oz self-raising flour, sieved

125g pack of honey roast ham, chopped

1 small onion, finely chopped

70g/2½oz desiccated coconut

326g can of sweetcorn, drained

Vegetable oil, for frying

Salt and freshly ground black pepper

1 Beat the milk, Greek yogurt, eggs and flour in a bowl to make a smooth batter.

2 Season, then mix in the ham, onion, coconut and sweetcorn.

3 Heat the oil in a frying pan. Put large dessertspoonfuls of the batter into the pan and fry for about 2 minutes on each side.

the asda chefs say...

To make a vegetarian version, just leave out the ham and add a bunch of spring onions, roughly chopped.

Yvonne Law
Epsom Downs, Surrey

I've always loved cooking and adapting recipes to surprise my family. I like to try new and interesting combinations of ingredients, which is how this recipe came about. I've got more time to experiment in the kitchen now that my three children have left home – fortunately they've all inherited my love of food, so now it's my turn to enjoy their culinary creations!

Preparing: 15 mins

 Cooking: 25 mins

 Serves 3

 Gluten free

baked frittata

This oven-baked omelette is so quick and easy, you can whip it up with whatever you have in your fridge

Ingredients

1tsp butter

2 plum tomatoes, sliced and deseeded

3 large mushrooms, sliced

3 rashers bacon, diced

2 spring onions, sliced

115g/4oz mild Cheddar cheese, grated

6 eggs

2tbsp milk

1½tsp dried mixed herbs

Salt and freshly ground black pepper

1 Preheat the oven to 180C/350F/Gas 4.

2 Grease a 20cm/8in flan dish with the butter, then layer the tomatoes, mushrooms, bacon and spring onions in it. Season well and top with the cheese.

3 In a small bowl, beat together the eggs and milk, then stir in the herbs. Pour over the other ingredients in the dish and bake for 25 minutes, or until golden.

the asda chefs say...

Try using cooked potato instead of the tomatoes and mushrooms.

Deborah Jackson

Blackburn, Lancashire

I feel that cold winter evenings warrant a warming meal, and this is the perfect time-saving recipe for busy people. You can use whatever ingredients you have to hand, and you simply put everything in the oven rather than frying it in a pan. I like to serve wedges of it with crusty bread and garlic butter or with a jacket potato and side salad. It's also tasty at breakfast time.

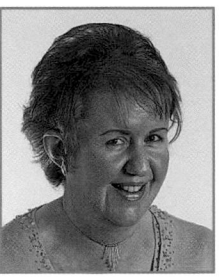

lancashire beef crumble

This is a real winter warmer and will go down a treat with all the family. Very good value, it's also quick to prepare – just pop it in the oven and put your feet up

 Preparing: 5 mins

 Cooking: 1 hour

 Serves 4

 Ideal TV dinner

Ingredients

1 onion, finely chopped

455g/1lb minced beef

115g/4oz button mushrooms, roughly chopped

115ml/4fl oz beef stock made from 1tsp beef concentrate

1tbsp Worcestershire sauce

Salt and freshly ground black pepper

For the crumble

30g/1oz butter

115g/4oz plain flour

55g/2oz Lancashire cheese, grated or crumbled

1 Preheat the oven to 200C/400F/Gas 6. Fry the onion, beef and mushrooms for 5 minutes in a large non-stick pan.

2 Add the beef stock and Worcestershire sauce and season. Cover the pan and simmer for 30 minutes.

3 Meanwhile, put the butter and the flour in a food processor and mix until it resembles breadcrumbs. If you don't have a food processor, rub the butter into the flour with your fingertips. Fold in the grated cheese.

4 Put the beef into a shallow ovenproof dish and cover with the crumble mixture. Bake for 25 minutes until golden.

the asda chefs say...

For a richer flavour, add 100ml/3½fl oz red wine, 3tbsp tomato purée and 1tsp dried mixed herbs to the beef and use 100ml less water to make up the stock. Cheddar cheese works just as well as the traditional Lancashire, and why not add 1tsp of dried mixed herbs to the crumble.

Christine Davey
Asda Colleague, Ashford

This recipe was given to me about 20 years ago by a relative, and I'm still making it, although it's changed a little bit over the years. My kids loved it when they were at school – all their friends would want to come around whenever we were having it. I do enjoy cooking but I work full-time, as an events co-ordinator at Asda Ashford. I don't really get the time to cook as much as I'd like to, but these days there's such a big variety of ready-prepared foods available, so I take advantage of that. I really like the Asda Fresh range, because you still feel like you're doing part of the cooking yourself, but you don't have to do all the preparation!

cheesy muffins

Spicy Worcestershire sauce adds a real tang to this tasty version of Welsh rarebit topped with bacon

 Preparing: 5 mins

 Cooking: 15 mins

 Serves 4

 Ideal snack

Ingredients

8 rashers streaky bacon

225g/8oz mature Cheddar cheese, grated

30g/1oz butter, softened

1tbsp Worcestershire sauce

1tbsp English mustard

2tbsp beer

4 muffins, halved

Apple or tomato chutney, to serve

1 Preheat the grill, then cook the bacon for 6-8 minutes, turning halfway through, until crispy.

2 In a small bowl, mix the cheese, butter, Worcestershire sauce, mustard and beer together.

3 Toast the muffins and spread with the cheese mixture. Grill until the cheese has melted and turned golden. Top with the bacon and serve with apple or tomato chutney.

the asda chefs say...

Use bread if you haven't got any muffins, just keep your eye on it to make sure it doesn't burn.

David Martin
Haworth, West Yorkshire

I learned to cook when I was at university — it was either that or starve. I'm a good old-fashioned Englishman, give me a traditional roast dinner anytime. I think these tasty little snacks include the best of British — muffins, cheese and bacon, not to mention Worcestershire sauce and English mustard. I always think that locally-produced ingredients taste the best, so my top tip is buy British!

Preparing: 10 mins

 Cooking: 15 mins

 Serves 4

 Gluten free

Ingredients

910g/2lb mashed potatoes

170g/6oz mix of carrots and swede, diced and boiled

60g/2oz half-fat red Leicester cheese, grated

Salt and freshly ground black pepper

1 Preheat the grill until hot. Mix all the ingredients, reserving half the cheese, in a large basin. Divide the mixture into 8 and shape into burgers. Put in the freezer for 15 minutes.

2 Grill for 5-7 minutes on each side until the burgers are golden brown. Sprinkle over the remaining cheese, grill to melt and serve with mixed vegetables and fried red onions.

potato burgers

Great for those who don't eat meat, this idea was created out of a need to use up surplus vegetables

the asda chefs say...

This is a great way to get kids to eat vegetables. For a tasty variation, add 2 chopped spring onions, 1 crushed garlic clove and 2tbsp chopped fresh herbs.

Andrew Whiteman
Nuneaton, Warwickshire

My wife and I became vegetarian after our daughter was born 12 years ago. I don't miss meat at all. In fact, I think I've had a wider variety of food since becoming a vegetarian than I did when I used to eat meat. I've eaten a lot of things that I would never have tried before – the other night we had a meal that had nine different vegetables on the plate!

gingerbread trifle

Spicy gingernut biscuits are the secret ingredient.
Everyone loves this dessert — especially kids

 Preparing: 10 mins

 No cooking required

 Serves 4-6

 2 hours chilling

Ingredients

284ml pot of whipping cream

30g/1oz caster sugar.

298g can of Healthy Choice mandarin segments

300g/10½oz ginger nut biscuits, each one broken into about 5 pieces

1 chocolate flake, crumbled to decorate

1 Whip the cream with the sugar until it forms soft peaks.

2 Drain the mandarins, reserving 2tbsp of the juice. Place half the biscuits into individual glass dishes; cover with half the mandarins and the reserved juice.

3 Cover with half the cream, and then start again – biscuits, mandarins and ending with cream. Cover and chill for 2 hours. Decorate with the crumbled flake before serving.

Janet Foster
Catwick, East Yorkshire

About 10 years ago, I decided to go back to school and take a Cook's Professional Certificate at Bishop Burton College. It was my tutor who suggested I try setting up an outside catering business and I've never looked back. I've been making this dessert for over 25 years for my own family and now it's just as popular with my clients – whether it's for a wedding, a funeral or an office party!

the asda chefs say...
Drizzle a little orange liqueur such as Grand Marnier or Cointreau over the biscuits for a boozy taste.

banoffi pie

The sticky toffee filling, bananas and cream make this a pudding that everyone will want second helpings of

Ingredients

100g/3½oz butter

200g/7oz digestive biscuits, crushed

397g can of condensed milk

284ml pot of double cream

3 bananas sliced

1tsp instant coffee powder

1tbsp caster sugar

1 chocolate flake, crumbled

1 Melt the butter and mix with the digestives. Press the mixture into individual glass dishes. Put in the freezer for 10-15 minutes.

2 In a small saucepan, simmer the condensed milk over a medium heat, stirring constantly, until it has turned a toffee colour. Take off the heat and cool.

3 Add 2-3tbsp of the cream to the toffeed milk, then pour it over the biscuit base. Cut the bananas into 1cm/½in slices and arrange on top of the toffee.

4 Whip the cream, coffee and sugar together, spread over the bananas and top with the flake. Chill for 30 minutes and serve.

Jane Porter

Pontypool, Torfaen

This was the first thing that I ever made for my fiancé. We are both big rugby fans and met watching a match in a pub and managed to hit it off, despite supporting different teams. When he first came to visit me in Cheshire, I made this dessert for him as I knew he had a sweet tooth. Two months later we were engaged. They say the way to a man's heart is though his stomach. It certainly worked for me!

girls' night in

A few bottles of wine, more than few laughs and loads of gossip… the only thing missing is the food. The recipes in this chapter will let you push the boat out a bit without breaking the bank and most of them can be prepared in advance, so you'll be free to enjoy the evening just as much as your girlfriends. There are some delicious salads and low-fat recipes (you'll find some more in the 'Got to be Good' chapter), lots of nibbles and a hopelessly irresistible chocolate truffle cake!

feta crostini

These tasty little toasts are packed full of flavour and make a deliciously different snack to have with drinks

 Preparing: 10 mins

 Cooking: 2 mins

 Serves 6

 Vegetarian dish

Ingredients

1 French loaf, sliced

1 garlic clove, halved

2tbsp extra virgin olive oil

8oz pitted black olives

100g/3½oz Greek yogurt

115g/4oz feta cheese, roughly chopped

2tbsp freshly chopped mint, plus extra leaves to garnish

Cucumber slices, to garnish

1 Toast the bread on both sides and rub with the garlic, then drizzle over half the olive oil.

2 Whizz the olives with the rest of the oil in a food processer and spread onto the toast.

3 Mix together the yogurt, feta cheese and mint, and spoon it onto the olive paté.

4 Top with the cucumber slices and a few extra mint leaves.

the asda chefs say...

Add some chopped roasted red peppers or sun-dried tomatoes for extra flavour.

Rebecca Taylor
Manchester

I'm a pretty adventurous cook and I'm always looking for new ideas. These toasts were inspired by a holiday in Greece, but I love Italian food and curries as well. I've got my mum to thank for a lot of my cooking skills – she taught me the basics, but there have been mistakes along the way. When I was very young I once tried to boil some potatoes without water!

Preparing: 5 mins

 Cooking: 20 mins

 Serves 4

 Gluten free

salmon with prawns

Serve this luxurious dish on special occasions – it's foolproof, delicious and bound to impress

Ingredients

4 salmon steaks

Juice of half a lemon

142ml pot of single cream

250g/9oz cooked, peeled prawns

Salt and freshly ground black pepper

1 Preheat oven to 190C/375F/ Gas 5.

2 Put each salmon steak on a piece of baking parchment, season and add a little lemon juice. Fold over the baking parchment to close the parcels and bake for about 20 minutes.

3 While the salmon is cooking, put the cream in a saucepan, season well and heat gently until it thickens slightly. Take off the heat and add the prawns.

4 Serve the salmon with the sauce and seasonal vegetables.

the asda chefs say...

Lemon juice reacts with aluminium foil, so make sure you only use baking parchment to make the parcels.

Joyce Kelly
Plymouth, Devon

When cooking salmon in the oven, it's important to keep an eye on it – if you over-cook it, it will dry out – but it's hard to give a definitive time for oven-baking, because much depends on the type of oven that you're using and the thickness of the salmon fillet. Salmon is cooked when it starts to flake, so the first time you make this dish, check the salmon after 15 minutes and keep an eye on it.

warm mushroom salad

Jonathan's salad can be served as either a starter or a main course. Stuff the mushrooms with creamy cheese and serve with crisp salad leaves and crusty bread

 Preparing: 10 mins

 Cooking: 12-14 mins

 Serves 6

 Gluten free

Ingredients

250g pack of jumbo mushrooms – there are usually 6 in a pack

Juice of 1 lemon

2 x 100g packs of soft goats' cheese logs

3tbsp double cream

½tsp Dijon mustard

2 large beef tomatoes, thinly sliced

1tbsp extra virgin olive oil

40g bag of fresh rocket

Salt and freshly ground black pepper

1 Preheat the oven to 180C/350F/Gas 4.

2 Cut a thin slice off the round side of each mushroom so it sits level. Trim the stalks. Season the mushrooms and brush the inside of each one with lemon juice.

3 Make the filling by mixing the goats' cheese, cream, mustard and seasoning until smooth. Spoon it into the cavity of the mushrooms and smooth off until level. Top with a slice of tomato and drizzle over a little olive oil. Bake for 12-14 minutes, basting occasionally with the juices.

4 Put the mushrooms on serving plates and top with the rocket leaves. Grind over some black pepper and serve.

chef's secret...
Jonathan Moore
Asda innovation chef

The mushroom is quite soft and smooth, so it's good with a contrasting texture, such as crusty garlic bread. The mushrooms make quite a filling, 'meaty' salad. If you're short of time, buy 455g/1lb of different mushrooms, such as chestnut, oyster and field, slice them and sauté in 85g/3oz butter. Serve on toasted French stick or ciabatta with salad.

warm salads

Warm salads must always be assembled just before you are ready to serve it, otherwise the warm ingredients will cause the delicate salad leaves to wilt. Ingredients that work well with a green salad are crispy lardons (cubes of bacon), croûtons, warm pasta, potatoes, mushrooms or chunks of chicken.

tuscany tarts

With lots of mouthwatering Mediterranean flavours, these puff pastry tarts are a great summer starter

 Preparing: 20 mins

 Cooking: 15 mins

 Serves 8

 Vegetarian dish

Ingredients

455g/1lb puff pastry

2tbsp tomato purée

15g pack of fresh basil

4 tomatoes, sliced

285g jar of artichoke hearts or roasted bell peppers, drained and sliced

30g/1oz Parmesan cheese, grated

1 small jar of pitted black olives

Freshly ground black pepper

1 Preheat the oven to 220C/425F/ Gas 7. Roll out the puff pastry on a lightly floured surface and cut into 13cm/5in circles.

2 Put the pastry onto a non-stick baking sheet, spread over the tomato purée. Add a few basil leaves, then add the tomatoes and artichokes or peppers. Season, sprinkle over the cheese and olives and bake for 15 minutes.

3 Serve immediately garnished with torn basil leaves and salad.

the asda chefs say...

For a fishy version, add some chopped anchovies.

Diana Hancock
Ilkley, West Yorkshire

My husband and I were on holiday in Tuscany in the mid 1970's and one day we went into a little family-run restaurant. My meal was absolutely delicious and so I said to the waiter that it was superb. He disappeared into the kitchen and came out with his grandmother, an old Italian lady grinning from ear to ear. She gave me a tour of her kitchen – and the recipe!

Preparing: 35 mins

 Cooking: 10-15 mins

 Serves 4

 Milk and gluten free

salmon kyoto

The salmon can be cooked under the grill or on a barbecue for a delicious chargrilled flavour

Ingredients

2tbsp light soy sauce

2tbsp orange juice

2tbsp sunflower oil

2tbsp tomato ketchup

2 small spring onions, finely chopped

1 garlic clove, crushed

1tbsp lemon juice

½tsp minced ginger

½tsp English mustard

4 salmon steaks or fillets

3 spring onions, sliced lengthwise

1 Make the marinade by putting the first nine ingredients into a screwtop jar and shaking well.

2 Put the fish into a non-metallic dish and pour over the marinade, reserving 1tbsp. Leave to stand for 30 minutes, turning once.

3 Preheat the grill. Drain the salmon, discarding the marinade. Cook for 10-15 minutes, depending on its thickness, brushing with the reserved marinade and turning halfway through. Serve garnished with the sliced spring onions.

Audrey Hughes
Dundee, Tayside

About 10 years ago while living in the USA, we bought a barbecue and a version of this recipe was included in the book of instructions.

Salmon wasn't very popular with my family at the time, but this converted them. I'm lucky living where I do as we get wonderful fish on the fresh fish counter at our local Asda – it's encouraged me to try lots of new things.

mini pesto pancakes

A bit of pesto can transform an everday pancake into something really yummy. Topped with cream cheese, salmon and pine nuts, these little ones are wickedly rich, but surprisingly simple to make

 Preparing: 30 mins

 Cooking: 10 mins

 Serves 6 as a starter

 Great for buffets

Ingredients

For the pancakes

115g/4oz self-raising flour

150ml/5fl oz milk

1 egg

2tbsp pesto

1tsp vegetable oil, plus extra for frying

Freshly ground black pepper

For the topping

100g tub of soft cream cheese

2 x 100g packs of smoked salmon, cut into strips

30g/1oz pine nuts, toasted

1 pot of fresh growing basil

1 Sieve the flour into a bowl and season with pepper. Add half the milk, the egg and the pesto and whisk until the mixture forms a smooth batter. Add the remaining milk and whisk until evenly blended. Allow to rest in the fridge for 15 minutes then add a teaspoon of vegetable oil to the mixture.

2 Heat a large, flat frying pan and brush with a little oil. Put teaspoons of the mixture into the pan, 3 or 4 at a time. Allow 30 seconds for the pancakes to rise, then flip them over and cook briefly on the other side. Continue until all the mixture is used up – you should have about 25 mini pancakes.

3 Arrange the pancakes on a plate and top each one with a small spoonful of cream cheese, a piece of salmon, a few pine nuts and a basil leaf.

the asda chefs say...

Be careful when toasting the pine nuts. Dry fry them in a flat-bottomed pan for a minute or two, but keep shaking the pan and keep a close eye on them to stop them from burning. You won't need to add any salt as there is enough in the pesto and smoked salmon. The pancakes can be made well in advance then frozen for up to 3 months and assembled when you're ready to eat them.

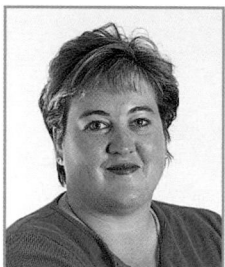

Della Moore
West Bridgford, Nottinghamshire

This recipe was developed with a little help from a friend and my sister! My friend and I were playing with a blini recipe and were inspired by my sister's pasta recipes to add pesto to the pancake mixture. My friend and I are part of social cookery group – there are about nine of us who regularly meet up to share ideas. We regularly hold "fuddles" at each other's houses – they're a great chance to swap recipes and to socialise. We all bring a new or favourite dish along for everyone else to try, along with a few glasses of wine, of course.

vegetable lasagne

There's nothing quite like a lasagne for feeding the hungry hordes. This version might be meat-free, but it's still full of flavour and it's great if you're on a budget, too – you can use whatever veg you have in the fridge!

 Preparing: 30 mins

 Cooking: 1 hour

 Serves 6

 Vegetarian dish

Ingredients

455g/1lb carrots, peeled and roughly chopped

1tbsp vegetable oil

455g/1lb onions, roughly chopped

250g pack of mushrooms, roughly chopped

1 red pepper, de-seeded, roughly chopped

400g can of plum tomatoes

2tbsp tomato purée

2tsp dried mixed herbs

1tsp garlic purée

2 x 35g packets of four cheese sauce mix

600ml/1pint skimmed milk

375g pack of dried lasagne

30g/1oz Parmesan cheese, grated

115g/4oz mature Cheddar cheese, grated

Salt and freshly ground black pepper

1 Preheat the oven to 190C/375F/Gas 5. Boil the carrots until tender, then drain and mash them.

2 Heat the oil in a large frying pan, gently fry the onions, mushrooms and red pepper until softened.

3 Add the carrots to the onion mixture, along with the tomatoes, tomato purée, herbs and garlic purée. Season and simmer gently for 20 minutes. While this is cooking, make up the sauce with the milk.

4 Spoon some of the vegetable sauce into an ovenproof dish, cover with lasagne sheets and spoon over some cheese sauce. Continue layering in this way until all the ingredients have been used, finishing with the cheese sauce.

5 Sprinkle over the Parmesan and Cheddar cheeses and bake for 30 minutes until golden. Allow to stand for 5 minutes before cutting.

the asda chefs say...

For a nice change, replace the carrots with sweet potato, swede or parsnip. This can be made in advance and frozen, either cooked or uncooked. You can reduce the calories by using half-fat cheese.

Phyllis Maltby
Whitemoor, Nottingham

Two of my children are vegetarian and this is one of the dishes I made for them in the days before things like microwaves and ready-meals were available, and I still make it for myself. It freezes well (cooked or uncooked) and I sometimes reheat it in the microwave if I'm in a hurry. I try to cook most nights and as a rule, I enjoy it. I get lots of ideas from things I've seen on cookery programmes and I'm not afraid to give new ideas a try or make things up from scratch. Generally speaking, I think good, home-cooked food is far superior to what's served in restaurants.

cheesy dip

Dips make a tasty nibble at the start of the evening – this one is a bit like a fondue, but without the fuss

 Preparing: 5 mins

 Cooking: 30 mins

 Serves 6

 Gluten free

Ingredients

1 garlic clove, crushed

340g/12oz red Leicester cheese, grated

340g/12oz Gruyère or Emmenthal cheese, grated

1tbsp tomato purée

150ml/5fl oz semi-skimmed milk or white wine, reserving 3tbsp

2tsp cornflour or 1 large egg, beaten

1 Preheat the oven to 230C/450F/ Gas 8.

2 Mix the garlic into the cheeses and put in an ovenproof dish. Stir the tomato purée into the milk or wine, pour over the cheese and bake for 15 minutes until melted, stirring occasionally.

3 Mix the cornflour or egg into the reserved liquid, stir into the cheese mixture and bake for a further 15 minutes until cooked.

4 Allow the dip to cool for a few minutes before serving with crusty bread sticks or crudités.

the asda chefs say...

To make this hotter, add 2tbsp sliced jalapeño peppers or 2 sliced red chillies.

Lynsey Parker
Sprotbrough, South Yorkshire

I love to try out new recipes and I think I'm a pretty good cook. My boyfriend's appetite has increased since knowing me, so I take that as a good sign! Most of my recipes have been passed down through the family, and I was taught to cook by my grandma and my mum. This recipe is an old family secret I got from my boyfriend's Italian grandmother. I love cheese, so it's one of my favourites!

baked salmon

This is a fresh, colourful dish that tastes great and is healthy too – perfect for when the girls get together

 Preparing: 5 mins

 Cooking: 15 mins

 Serves 4

 Gluten free

Ingredients

4 salmon fillets

Half a whole nutmeg

15g/½oz butter, diced

15g pack fresh dill, chopped, plus a few sprigs to garnish

8tbsp natural yogurt

Salt and freshly ground black pepper

1 Preheat oven to 200C/400F/ Gas 6.

2 Put the salmon in a large oven-proof dish. Grate over the nutmeg and divide the butter over the top of each fillet. Season and bake for 15 minutes.

3 Near the end of the cooking time, mix the chopped dill and yogurt and gently heat in a small saucepan for a few minutes. Pour over the salmon and garnish with fresh dill. Serve with boiled potatoes, courgettes and carrots.

the asda chefs say...

Watercress can be used instead of dill – it works just as well.

Ingrid Chapman
Gosport, Hampshire

I have a large collection of cookery books and I'm forever cutting out recipes from newspapers and magazines, too. Friends tease me and ask if I really make all these things, but generally I do, if only once! Fish is a favourite in our house, but I tend to stick to salmon fillets, tuna steaks and prawns – to be honest, I don't like my fish with the head and tail on!

caesar salad

Neil's recipe for a basic Caesar salad can be made in minutes using things that most of us have in the fridge. Add whatever takes your fancy to make it into more of a meal that's perfect for outdoor summertime eating

 Preparing: 15 mins

 Cooking: 6-8 mins

 Serves 4 as a starter

 Light but tasty

Ingredients

1 small baguette

3 garlic cloves

3tbsp olive oil

2 anchovy fillets

142ml pot of sour cream

Juice of half a lemon

2 romaine or cos lettuces, 4 little gems, or 1 iceberg lettuce

115g/4oz freshly grated Parmesan cheese, plus 30g/1oz in one piece

Salt and freshly ground black pepper

1 Preheat the oven to 200C/400F/Gas 6.

2 Make the croûtons by cutting the baguette into large chunks. Squash 2 garlic cloves with their skins on and scatter them among the cut bread. Drizzle over 2tbsp of the oil and bake for 6-8 minutes until the bread is crisp and golden.

3 While the croûtons are in the oven, make the dressing. Using a pestle and mortar or a food processor, pound the anchovies and the remaining garlic clove into a paste. Season to taste then add the cream, lemon juice and remaining oil and mix well.

4 Pour the dressing into a large bowl, add the lettuce leaves and croûtons, then sprinkle over the grated Parmesan. Mix well. Make Parmesan shavings from the whole piece with a vegetable peeler. Arrange on the salad, grind over black pepper and serve.

chef's secret...
Neil Nugent
Asda innovation chef

Always grind black pepper just before serving – it will give a more intense taste as it's the cracking of the pepper that releases the natural oils and flavour.

snappy dressings

The only limit to making delicious dressings is your own imagination. As a base for a vinaigrette, start by mixing 2-3tbsp of olive oil, 1tbsp of balsamic vinegar; ½tsp Dijon mustard and seasoning. Then enhance it with some of your favourite flavours such as garlic, chillies, tomato pulp, honey or even raspberries. Or use lots of your favourite herbs – fresh, of course!

salmon gloria

Fresh, colourful and tasty, this is also very nutritious. Double or treble the recipe to cater for your friends

 Preparing: 5 mins

 Cooking: 10 mins

 Serves 2

 Milk and gluten free

Ingredients

2tbsp sunflower oil

1 large onion, finely sliced

2 salmon fillets

A pinch of ground ginger

1 large courgette, thinly sliced

8 cherry tomatoes

Juice of half a lemon

Lime wedges, to garnish

1 Heat the oil in a large frying pan and gently fry the onion for a few minutes, until it starts to go soft.

2 Add the salmon into the pan with onions, then add the ginger, courgettes, cherry tomatoes and lemon juice.

3 Cover and cook for about 8 minutes or until the salmon is cooked through.

4 Serve garnished with the lime wedges.

the asda chefs say...

For a fresh flavour, use root ginger, instead of powdered, if you have it.

Joan Amor
Wallington, Surrey

I'm always amazed by the glorious colours in the pan whenever I make this recipe, which is how it got its name – it's a favourite with my family and friends.

Sometimes I do get a little bit bored with making the same dish over and over again, so one trick I've learned is to never take a shopping list with me to my local Asda – instead I let their special offers decide my menus for me.

Preparing: 5 mins

 Cooking: 10 mins

 Serves 4

 Milk free

chicken pittas

Pitta breads are ideal for making quick snacks that you can eat with your hands without too much mess!

Ingredients

1tbsp olive oil

3 skinless chicken breasts, diced

½tsp garlic salt

70g can of tomato purée

4 large pitta breads, halved

Half an iceberg lettuce, shredded

Half a cucumber, sliced

8 cherry tomatoes, halved

1 Heat the oil in a frying pan, add the chicken and fry for 5 minutes, stir until cooked. Season to taste with garlic salt.

2 Stir in the tomato purée and cook for a further 3 minutes.

3 Cut the pitta breads down one side then toast, either in a toaster or under a grill, until golden brown.

4 Fill the pitta with the lettuce, cucumber, tomatoes and the chicken mixture and serve.

the asda chefs say...

Spice the chicken mixture with some finely chopped red chilli if you like it.

Emma Fox
Shoeburyness, Essex

I was off work for a while because of illness and got very bored. So I started messing about in the kitchen, trying out different recipes, and my interest in cookery just took off from there. Now I cook every weekend for my mum and brother and they really enjoy it. I like Gary Rhodes and Jamie Oliver, but when it comes to what I cook, I have a definite number one favourite, and that's chicken.

veggie pasta bake

Tasty and healthy, too, this is the perfect thing when friends come around and you don't want to be stuck in the kitchen. You can add what you like, making it a different dish every time!

 Preparing: 10 mins

 Cooking: 15 mins

 Serves 4-6

 Vegetarian dish

Ingredients

350g pack of dried pasta

2 x 400g cans of chopped tomatoes

2 vegetable stock cubes

3 assorted peppers, de-seeded and roughly chopped

1 large onion, finely chopped

1tsp dried oregano

2tsp crushed garlic

85g/3oz sliced button mushrooms

2tbsp tomato purée

6 cherry tomatoes, halved

1tsp cornflour

85g/3oz half fat Cheddar cheese, grated

55g/2oz Parmesan cheese, grated

Chopped fresh parsley, to garnish

Freshly ground black pepper

1 Cook the pasta according to the pack instructions. Drain and set aside.

2 Meanwhile, put the tomatoes into a large saucepan and crumble in the stock cubes. Add the peppers, onion, oregano and garlic and cook for 5 minutes. Preheat the grill.

3 Add the mushrooms, tomato purée and cherry tomatoes to the pan and cook for a further 5 minutes. Mix the cornflour with 2tsp cold water, season well and add it to the pan, stirring continually as the sauce thickens.

4 Mix the sauce with the drained pasta and put it in a large, shallow ovenproof dish. Sprinkle over the cheeses and put under the grill until golden brown and bubbling. Garnish with the chopped parsley and serve.

the asda chefs say...

For a change, use a jar of roasted peppers instead of the fresh peppers and 6 sun-dried tomatoes, roughly chopped, instead of cherry tomatoes. To make the topping crunchy, mix in 3tbsp dried breadcrumbs with the cheese.

Adele Moore
Gosport, Hampshire

I used to make this dish with sausages and bacon, so when I decided to go on a diet, I knew that I definitely had to change it. A few others at work were on a diet too, so we used to swap ideas for making things healthier – it can be hard adapting recipes to make them low in fat because you still want to have all the flavour. You can cook your vegetables with a stock cube, instead of frying them in oil. This recipe must have been pretty good because every time I made it for lunch and took it to work, all the others wanted some. The diet worked too – I lost three stones!

chocolate chestnut truffle cake

 Preparing: 20 mins

 No baking required

 Serves 12

 3 hours chilling

A really rich, chocolatey dessert is an essential part of a really good girls' night in – to make room for this one, choose a lighter main course. Go on, treat yourself!

Ingredients

255g/9oz butter

300g/10½oz digestive biscuits, crushed

225g/8oz plain chocolate, broken into pieces

435g can of sweetened chestnut purée

115g/4oz caster sugar

1 Line a 9in/23cm springform cake tin with foil. Melt 140g/5oz of the butter and mix it with the crushed digestives. Press the mixture firmly into the base of the tin. Pop into the freezer to chill for 20 minutes.

2 Set a large bowl over a pan of simmering water. Put the chocolate into the bowl and melt it gently for 10-15 minutes. Cut the remaining butter into cubes and stir it into the chocolate.

3 While the chocolate is melting, put the chestnut purée and caster sugar into a large bowl and beat, either with an electric mixer or by hand, until well mixed. Pour the melted chocolate mixture into the chestnut mixture and beat well.

4 Pour the filling onto the biscuit base and smooth the top. Chill in the fridge for 3 hours. Serve in thin slices as it's very rich.

the asda chefs say...

Cut through the richness of this dessert by serving it with some soft fruit, such as raspberries or strawberries. For an even quicker chestnut pudding, mix the purée gently with 600ml/1pint lightly whipped double cream and layer the mixture in a serving dish with a packet of crushed meringue nests. Top with grated chocolate and serve.

Wendy Jones-Bierton
Denmead, Hampshire

A while ago my daughter and I found out we couldn't tolerate dairy products. We love chocolate, but most chocolate cheesecakes have cream in them, so I wanted to invent one that was largely dairy-free. It took a bit of experimenting, but I found the chestnuts work perfectly. When I make it for us, I use soya spread instead of butter. I've got four children, so I watch the budget. I always laugh at those TV chefs who say 'use expensive chocolate with 70 per cent cocoa solids'. I use Smart Price products in this recipe and it still tastes delicious.

peggy borton's lemon curd dip

Everyone remembers lemon curd from their childhood, but here's a recipe for a grown-up dessert that's fresh and full of zingy flavour – and it's great for sharing!

 Preparing: 5 mins

 Cooking: 10 mins

 Serves 4

 Gluten free

Ingredients

Finely grated zest and
juice of 2 unwaxed lemons

1tbsp unsalted butter

2tbsp caster sugar

2 egg yolks

200g tub of half-fat
crème fraîche

340g/12oz mixed fresh
fruit, such as sliced
apples, strawberries,
cherries, pineapple or
passion fruit, to serve

1 Put the lemon zest and juice, butter, sugar and egg yolks into a saucepan and heat gently, stirring continuously, until everything is blended together and the mixture thickens. This could also be done in the microwave – heat on HIGH for 1 minute 20 seconds, whisking every 20 seconds. Allow to cool.

2 Mix the cooled lemon curd with the crème fraîche and serve it with the fruit as a dip.

Rosemarie Mann
Ampfield, Hampshire

The lemon curd recipe is from my mum – she seemed to be able to throw everything into the pan and it always came out perfectly. It's so fresh and light – you can have it on toast or in cakes or just on ice cream. I have to confess that I don't really like cooking – I can make nice meals when I try but my partner is a bit of a gobbler – he just eats the meal really quickly and asks what's next, so there's not much point in spending too much time on things. These days there are really good ready-made meals in Asda, so that's a good excuse for me to be lazy in the kitchen.

the asda chefs say...
For a twist on the lemon curd, use one lime and one lemon, instead of two lemons. You can freeze the leftover egg whites and use them later to make meringues.

quick ice cream

Here's a cheat's way to make ice cream – make it at the last minute and impress your friends

 Preparing: 5 mins

 No cooking required

 Serves 6

 Gluten free

Ingredients

300ml/10fl oz double cream

300ml/10fl oz Greek yogurt

3 meringue nests, crushed

500g pack of frozen summer fruits mix

1 Whip the cream until soft peaks form. Stir in the yogurt and crushed meringue nests.

2 Add the fruit, mixing it in well and serve – the frozen fruit will freeze the cream mixture to give a soft-set ice cream.

Marion Gough
Asda Colleague, Aberdare

Quick and easy are both important to me when it comes to cooking – I'm a working mum so I don't have ages to spend in the kitchen. My family likes things like quiches and lasagnes, so I think I've managed to perfect those. I usually prefer to make things from scratch and I like to use as many fresh ingredients as possible – they taste nicer and are better value, too.

the asda chefs say...
If you're feeling really indulgent, serve this with warm chocolate sauce – make the chocolate pots recipe on page 101, but don't let the mixture set.

Preparing: 5 mins

 No cooking required

 Serves 4

 5 hours chilling

low-fat tiramisù

A low-fat recipe that still feels really indulgent. Save your calorie allowance for a glass of wine – and enjoy!

Ingredients

200g tub of half-fat crème fraîche

250g tub of quark

20g/⅔oz Canderel or similar sweetener

20 Boudoir biscuits

Half a teacup of strong coffee, cooled

1tbsp cocoa powder

1 Mix together the crème fraîche, quark and Canderel.

2 Dip the sponge fingers in the coffee and layer them in a serving dish with the crème fraîche mix, ending with a crème fraîche layer.

3 Dust the top with the cocoa powder, then put the dish in the fridge to set for 5 hours.

the asda chefs say...

For an extra-boozy pud, replace some of the coffee with a coffee liqueur such as Kahlúa or Tia Maria. Trifle sponges work just as well as Boudoir biscuits.
Use strips of greaseproof paper when you're dusting with the cocoa powder to get the striped effect.

Chris Stanton
Luton, Bedfordshire

I used to go to Slimming World, where we were always trying to come up with low-fat, but tasty recipes. This is one that I've adapted from a recipe book – it really tastes like you're having something you shouldn't. I like to experiment with recipes but I have to admit that I'm a bit short-tempered in the kitchen – if things don't go to plan, they often end up thrown out in the back garden!

just the two of us

Cooking a special meal is one of the best ways of saying thank you to a life-long friend or partner, and it's also a great way to lure someone new into your life! This chapter contains lots of seductive secrets from the Asda chefs, including advice on how to cook the perfect steak. The recipes have been chosen to encourage you to be adventurous and splash out on the odd luxury ingredient. With the help of Asda's low prices, why not get a bottle of wine and some candles, too?

melon with orange

Simple, refreshing and inexpensive, this fruity starter is a brilliant way to kick off a light summertime meal

 Preparing: 20 mins

 No cooking required

 Serves 2

 Milk and gluten free

Ingredients

1 ripe melon

55g/2oz caster sugar

Juice of half a lemon

Juice and finely grated zest of 1 orange

6 mint leaves, chopped

1 Cut the melon into rough chunks or scoop out melon balls. Sprinkle over the sugar, lemon and orange juice and orange zest.

2 Leave for 15 minutes so the melon absorbs the flavours. Just before serving stir in the chopped mint.

Norma Timson
Harrogate, North Yorkshire

I love cooking and I especially love puddings. If I'm having people for dinner I don't just do one, I'll do three! I have had a few disasters in my kitchen – once I was making bread and put 16 times too much yeast in it. Each time I checked on it when it was rising, it had grown bigger and bigger – when it was ready to go in the oven I could hardly get my arms around it.

the asda chefs say...
Try using finely chopped preserved ginger and some ginger syrup instead of the orange zest and orange and lemon juice. Use whatever melon you like best, or mix two different types together

Preparing: 45 mins

 Cooking: 10 mins

 Serves 2

 Gluten free

mango-chilli salmon

A colourful dish that couldn't be simpler, this dish is a sure-fire way to get compliments from your partner

Ingredients

1 small ripe mango, peeled and chopped

Half a red chilli, deseeded and finely chopped

Juice of 1 lime

2 salmon fillets

1dsp olive oil

Knob of butter

1 Preheat oven to 180C/350F/ Gas 4. Mix the mango, chilli and lime juice, and pour over the salmon in a non-metallic bowl. Leave to marinate in the fridge for 30 minutes.

2 Heat the oil and butter in a frying pan and seal the salmon fillets for 30 seconds on each side. Transfer to an ovenproof dish and bake for 10 minutes.

3 Gently heat the marinade in the frying pan. Serve the salmon with the sauce, and mixed wild rice and vegetables.

the asda chefs say...

Don't marinate the fish for longer than 30 minutes.

Julia Havis
Colchester, Essex

I cook this all the time – it's really simple and it seems to impress the men! It's nice and spicy, but healthy too. I like to use fruit in my recipes – I probably came up with this on one of those days when I was using up what I had in my fridge. My local Asda in Colchester has every-thing I need including a great fish counter – they're all very friendly there so I always look forward to going.

gingerly fishcakes

Fishcakes are a great way to use fish and you can choose practically any variety – from good value canned tuna to fresh haddock or cod. The ginger adds a spicy flavour to these ones

 Preparing: 1 hour

 Cooking: 40 mins

 Serves 2

 Milk free

Ingredients

1 large baking potato, peeled and cut into cubes

5tbsp olive oil

1 onion, finely chopped

2½cm/1in piece of root ginger, peeled and finely grated

100g can of tuna in brine, drained and flaked

180g can of salmon, drained and flaked

100g pack of cooked, peeled prawns

1 egg, lightly beaten (optional)

4tbsp flour

Salt and freshly ground black pepper

1 Cook the potato for about 10 minutes or until soft in salted boiling water. Drain, mash and set aside to cool.

2 Heat 2tbsp of the olive oil and gently fry the onion and ginger for 15-20 minutes or until soft. Allow to cool for a moment, then add to the potato, along with the tuna, salmon and prawns, and the egg, if using. Season and mix well.

3 Shape the mixture into 6 small cakes and chill them in the fridge for about 45 minutes until firm.

4 Roll the fishcakes in the flour. Heat the remaining oil in a frying pan and shallow fry the fishcakes for 10 minutes, turning once. Serve immediately with green salad and mayonnaise.

the asda chefs say...

These fishcakes can be made in advance, then heated through in the oven at 190C/375F /Gas 5. For a fresh flavour, add the grated zest of half a lemon or lime, 2tbsp freshly chopped parsley and ½ tsp Dijon mustard.

Debra Sutton
North Ferriby, East Yorkshire

I don't eat meat but I love fish, so I suppose I'm a fisheterian! I really love a simple tuna steak, and monkfish is delicious, too. My specialty is bouillabaisse – a fish stew you can put anything and everything into. I love to travel and try different kinds of food – my favourite place is Italy so I do make lots of Italian-style things – lovely salads and pasta. My mother was a very good cook and my sister teaches at college so you could say that a love of cooking runs in our family. I have a few tricks up my sleeve, too, so if something goes wrong in the kitchen I just improvise.

cooking the perfect steak

Jonathan Moore
Asda innovation chef

"There's nothing quite like a juicy steak to get my mouth watering and yet it's one of the quickest and simplest things you can cook. The secret to steak is what you serve it with – sometimes I'm in the mood for a rich sauce, other times I just love a good old steak sandwich with loads of ketchup or a large dollop of mustard!"

1 Choosing the right cut of meat is important. Fillet is the best, most tender and most succulent cut and it needs the least cooking. It's suitable for frying or grilling and larger pieces can be roasted whole, but don't overcook it. Sirloin is a good-quality steak that's best for frying, grilling or barbecuing. Rump is cheaper than fillet but still tasty, and it's also good for frying, grilling and barbecuing.

2 Cooking steak couldn't be simpler. The classic way is to cook it rare, with the outside sealed and brown and the inside pink and juicy. A lot of people prefer it medium, with the inside cooked most of the way through. The most important thing is to cook it quickly, adding it to a hot pan, so the juices can be sealed in. Before you put it in the pan, season it lightly with salt and leave it for 20 minutes, then pat it dry with a paper towel – you'll get a crispier outside to the steak.

3 There are lots of great steak dishes – most of them involve a simply cooked steak with a delicious sauce. One of the most popular is pepper steak, in which the meat is coated with crushed peppercorns before cooking. A classic garnish for steak is pan-fried flat mushrooms, lightly grilled beef tomatoes and fresh watercress. Flavoured butters are also great with steak – parsley butter is delicious, but other options are chilli butter, peppercorn butter or horseradish butter. If you fancy a different accompaniment, add some Dijon mustard to mayonnaise with lots of chives. Or try roasting a double fillet steak in the oven, slicing it thinly and serving with a red wine sauce. For a classic steak sandwich, use thin sirloin steak, seared and piled on toasted bread with loads of fried onions and ketchup.

cooking times

A steak should be fried for 1-2 minutes on each side over a high heat to seal in the juices. Then the heat should be reduced to medium and the steaks cooked for 4-5 minutes (rare), 6-8 minutes (medium-rare) or 9-11 minutes (well done). These figures are for steaks about 2cm/¾in thick. For thicker steaks, allow an extra 3-4 minutes of cooking. It's best not to cook more than two steaks at a time. After cooking, allow your steak to rest for a few minutes before eating – this will help ensure that the meat re-absorbs its juices.

soy-glazed fillet of beef

The sticky soy glaze in this recipe has a rich flavour that's a perfect match for the beef. Serve with a nice red wine, sit back and wait for the compliments…

Ingredients

50ml/2fl oz soy sauce

1tbsp olive oil

4 garlic cloves, crushed

4tbsp dry sherry

Half a lemon, sliced

½tsp coarse-grain mustard

2 x 170g/6oz fillet steaks

Freshly ground black pepper

1 Preheat the oven to 220C/425F/Gas 7.

2 Combine the soy sauce, olive oil, garlic, sherry, lemon slices and mustard in a bowl. Lay the steaks in a non-metallic dish. Season with pepper, pour over the marinade and leave for at least 10 minutes. If you have time, leave the meat to marinate in the fridge for up to 4 hours.

3 Drain the steaks, reserving the marinade. Cook the meat on a rack in the oven for between 4 and 8 minutes, depending on how well-cooked you like your steak.

4 Remove the steaks from the oven and cover to keep them warm while they rest for a few minutes. Meanwhile, heat the marinade until it's bubbling and reduced slightly. Season the steaks and serve them with the sauce poured over.

the asda chefs say…

The timings for cooking the meat will depend a little on how thick your steak is. If it's more than 2.5cm/1in thick, allow an extra minute or two.

Sandra Holden
Middleton, Manchester

I've been involved with catering for a long time now – I was apprenticed to learn how to cook school meals. These days I work at a private nursery for children from six months to four years. This involves producing a wide range of ethnic dishes as well as meals for children with special dietary needs. At home, my husband and I share the cooking – it's usually a matter of who gets home from work first. What we decide to make often just depends on our mood and what we've got in the fridge at the time! This recipe's a good one for special occasions.

herby chicken tagliatelle

 Preparing: 5 mins

 Cooking: 20-25 mins

 Serves 2

 Easy main course

The dried herbs and the cider give this simple chicken and pasta dish a French-style flavour – a really good choice for people with big appetites!

Ingredients

1tbsp dried mixed herbs

2 small skinless chicken breasts

2tbsp olive oil

115g/4½oz mushrooms, sliced thinly

250ml/9fl oz dry white cider

300g pack of fresh tagliatelle

284ml pot of double cream

15g packet of fresh chives, roughly chopped

Freshly ground black pepper

1 Preheat the oven to 190C/375F/Gas 5.

2 Sprinkle the herbs onto a plate and roll the chicken breasts in them to coat. Heat 1tbsp oil in a frying pan and lightly brown the chicken on both sides, being careful not to burn the herb coating. Transfer the chicken to an ovenproof dish and cook in the oven for 20 minutes. Cover the chicken breasts with foil and allow to rest for a few minutes while you make the sauce.

3 Fry the mushrooms in the rest of the oil until softened. Add the cider and reduce until only a couple of tablespoons of liquid remain.

4 Meanwhile, cook the tagliatelle according to the pack instructions.

5 Add the cream to the mushrooms and heat through. Season, then stir into the cooked tagliatelle. Add the chives. Slice the chicken and arrange on the tagliatelle. Serve with asparagus spears.

the asda chefs say...

If you don't have any cider in the house, use apple juice, white wine or vermouth instead. To save time, use cooked chicken breasts — just slice and stir through the sauce until it's all hot.

Raymond James
Newport, Wales

This is a real favourite in our house – the kids love it. It's great because it's a good family dish, but it's also the kind of thing that you could serve at a dinner party. Cooking's like a hobby for me. My wife cooks during the week and I take over at weekends when I've got more time. I watch an awful lot of TV cookery programmes, and love things like *Ready Steady Cook* because you can pick up a lot of ideas. But I'm not a Delia type of cook: her approach is too fussy for me. I'm definitely more of a 'throw it all together' type.

broccoli and walnut lasagne

If you're tired of serving the same old thing, surprise your partner with this delectably different vegetable lasagne variation – this recipe serves four, and can be frozen, too

 Preparing: 10 mins

 Cooking: 1 hour

 Serves 4

 Vegetarian dish

Ingredients

250g pack of fresh lasagne or a 250g pack of Smart Price dried lasagne

3tbsp olive oil

1 large onion, roughly chopped

1 garlic clove, crushed

2 x 310g packs of broccoli, cut into florets

1tsp dried mixed herbs

150ml/5fl oz white wine (optional)

400g can of tomatoes

115g/4oz shelled walnuts, roughly chopped

30g/1oz margarine

30g/1oz plain flour

1tsp dried mustard

500ml/18fl oz milk

170g/6oz Cheddar cheese, grated

Salt and freshly ground black pepper

1 Cook the lasagne according to the pack instructions and drain. Preheat the oven to 200C/400F/Gas 6.

2 Heat the oil in a saucepan and sauté the onion until slightly soft. Add the garlic, broccoli, herbs and wine, if using, or 150ml water.

3 Add the tomatoes and season. Cover and simmer for 15-20 minutes, then stir in the walnuts.

4 Make the cheese sauce. In a saucepan, melt the margarine, add the flour and mustard. Stir well and cook gently for 3 minutes. Gradually whisk in the milk, stirring until the sauce begins to boil and thicken. Stir in three-quarters of the cheese, saving the rest to sprinkle on top.

5 Layer the lasagne in an ovenproof dish, seasoning as you go. Start with the vegetable mix on the base, then the lasagne and sauce. Continue layering, finishing with a layer of sauce. Sprinkle with the remaining cheese and bake for 20 minutes until the top is golden and brown.

the asda chefs say...

If you like cheesy flavours, omit the tomatoes and make more cheese sauce adding an extra 15g/½oz margarine, 15g/½oz plain flour, 150ml/5fl oz milk and 55g/2oz cheese.

Gillian Humphreys
Pontyberem, Carmarthenshire

I'm not a vegetarian, but I really enjoy this lasagne recipe because it's so tasty and unusual. Occasionally, when I feel the need to 'get healthy', I eat just fruit and veg for a while, though Italian dishes, curries and other spicy foods are my real favourites. I live on my own and always make an effort to cook something special when friends or family come round. My sister is always my guinea pig when I'm trying out a new recipe! Now that I have a selection of herbs growing in my garden, I'd like to be more adventurous about using them at meal times.

simply smoked salmon

Neil Nugent
Asda innovation chef

'When I want to make my wife Rachel something special but still really quick and easy, I go for smoked salmon. Here are three of her favourite recipes, all serve two, use a 100g pack of salmon and can be made in a matter of minutes…

1. To really bring out the flavour of smoked salmon, serve it with a simple salsa verde (left). Just mix together 3tbsp of olive oil with a 15g pack each of fresh parsley, mint and basil, all roughly chopped. Then add a finely chopped red onion, 1tbsp of chopped capers, a clove of crushed garlic, four roughly chopped gherkins, 1tsp of Dijon mustard and the juice of half a lemon. Mix everything together well and serve the salsa with the salmon and some of your favourite bread, toasted. Simple!

2. For a quick lunch for two that takes less than 10 minutes to put together, crush a garlic clove and mix it with 100g/3½oz Greek yogurt. Stir in half a cucumber that's been peeled, halved lengthways and thinly sliced. Then add the juice of half a lemon and a few roughly chopped leaves of your favourite fresh herbs – basil, mint, chives or coriander all work well. Finally, stir in 1tbsp olive oil. Slit two pitta breads down the side, toast them and divide the pack of smoked salmon between the two. Fill them generously with the cucumber salad mixture and serve!

3. One of Rachel's favourite breakfasts is smoked salmon and scrambled eggs – it's so easy to make, I don't mind treating her all the time! Toast two bagels and keep them warm. Heat 2tbsp of double cream until it comes to the boil, then remove it from the heat and stir in three beaten eggs and a knob of butter. Heat gently until the eggs are set, then divide between the bagels. Top off with the smoked salmon – layer it liberally on the bagels and season with a sprinkling of freshly ground black pepper.

easy does it!

Smoked salmon is easy to use and ready to eat straight from the pack, so there's hardly any preparation involved. In fact, the less you do to it, the better. You don't really even need to add any seasoning, as salt is added to the fish during the smoking process. Smoked salmon goes perfectly with cream cheese in a sandwich, on crispbread or canapés. Or just eat it on it's own with a generous squeeze of lemon juice and a sprinkling of black pepper.

chicken wrapped in smoked salmon

Preparing: 20 mins

Cooking: 30 mins

Serves 2

Gluten free

Spend a little more and splash out on this special treat. Watercress adds a peppery taste, while the mascarpone cheese makes the sauce mouthwateringly creamy

Ingredients

2 skinless chicken breasts

100g pack of smoked salmon

225g/8oz watercress, roughly chopped, plus a few whole sprigs to garnish

142ml pot of single cream

55g/2oz mascarpone cheese

50ml/2fl oz white wine

Freshly ground black pepper

1 Preheat the oven to 180C/350F/Gas 4. Wrap the chicken in the salmon and put in an ovenproof dish.

2 Mix the watercress, cream, mascarpone, wine and seasoning in a bowl and pour over the chicken.

3 Bake in the oven for 30 minutes. Garnish with the extra watercress and serve with new potatoes and a selection of vegetables.

the asda chefs say...

The chicken will release some juices during cooking, so to make the sauce look more appealing, remove the chicken from the dish, then pour the sauce into a blender and whizz for a few seconds. If it's too thick, add a drop of water before serving.

Leanne Potter
Boston, Lincolnshire

I used to make this recipe with bacon, instead of smoked salmon, but I decided to try this variation and decided I liked it better than the original. The smoked salmon gives the chicken a lot of flavour and keeps the meat nice and moist, too. I really love cooking for other people and when I have guests round for dinner I always try to do something special – I'm happy to take ages cooking a meal for other people. I suppose I'm a pretty confident cook – I don't ever try things out beforehand and I haven't ever had any major failures – well not so far, anyway!

tandoori pork en croûte

 Preparing: 15 mins

 Cooking: 30 mins

 Serves 2

 Serve hot or cold

This delicious pork dish looks absolutely spectacular and the tandoori spice gives it a nice Indian taste. If there's any left over, take it on a picnic and eat it cold

Ingredients

425g/15oz pork fillet

225g/8oz pork sausage meat

2tsp tandoori spice

1 small onion, finely chopped

500g pack of puff pastry

1 egg

Salt and freshly ground black pepper

1 Preheat the oven to 220C/425F/Gas 7. Season the pork then fry for 1-2 minutes on each side in a hot non-stick frying pan to seal it. Allow to cool.

2 Mix the sausage meat with the tandoori spice and onion. Roll out the pastry to a rectangle the same length as the pork and 3 times as wide. Trim the edges of the pastry and spread the sausage meat mixture evenly over it, leaving a small gap around the edges.

3 Whisk the egg with 1tbsp water. Put the pork fillet on the pastry, brush the edges of the pastry with the egg and wrap it around the pork fillet, sealing the edges as you go. Slash the pastry at 2.5cm/1in intervals.

4 Brush the top of the pastry with the remaining egg mixture and bake for 25-30 minutes until golden and crisp. Serve in slices.

the asda chefs say...

Sealing the pork fillet first gives it a tasty brown crust. Add a grated Bramley apple and the finely grated zest of a lemon to the sausage mixture. Or substitute the sausage meat mixture with 4 Extra Special sausages with their skins removed.

Robert Watt
Ellon, Aberdeenshire

Many moons ago, I was a galley boy in the Navy and it was then that I discovered my love of food. I worked my way up to Catering Officer where I was able to start being a bit more inventive with cooking. This recipe was inspired by my travels around the world – it's a fine example of what the experts call 'fusion food' – the pork is English, the tandoori stuffing comes from my days in India and the 'en croûte' incorporates a bit of French cooking. I do the majority of the cooking at home in Aberdeenshire – my wife's probably not quite as adventurous as I am when it comes to food!

chicken en papillote

Unwrap the little parcels and you'll find a few simple ingredients have been transformed into a tasty treat

 Preparing: 10 mins

 Cooking: 12-18 mins

 Serves 2

 Milk and gluten free

Ingredients

1 small onion, sliced

1tbsp olive oil

2tbsp dark brown sugar

¼tsp Dijon mustard or ½tsp coarse-grain mustard (optional)

2 skinless chicken breasts

Salt and freshly ground black pepper

1 Preheat the oven to 200C/400F/ Gas 6.

2 Gently fry the onion in the oil for 5 minutes. Add the sugar and mustard. Cut 2 large squares of foil. Put a chicken breast on each one then top with half the onion mixture. Season well.

3 Seal the foil around the chicken and put the parcels into an ovenproof dish. Bake for 15-20 minutes. Unwrap carefully as the escaping steam will be hot. Serve with mashed potatoes and oven-roasted tomatoes.

the asda chefs say...

For a change, add 1tsp soy sauce, ¼tsp of lazy minced ginger and a dash of Tabasco or sweet chilli sauce.

Muriel Driver
West Caister, Norfolk

My husband and I do a lot of entertaining and I enjoy being creative with the menu. Now we mainly have themed evenings – perhaps Japanese, Chinese or Indian. My husband is interested in cooking, too. When he retired from his job, the two of us decided to do a vegetarian cookery course. We went one day a week for a year – it was a lot of hard work, but well worth it.

Preparing: 15 mins

 Cooking: 15-20 mins

 Serves 2

 Milk and gluten free

thai chicken curry

This piquant dish is easy to make from scratch, but to save time you could use ready-made curry paste

Ingredients

Half a red onion, roughly chopped

1 garlic clove, roughly chopped

2.5cm/1in piece of root ginger, roughly chopped

1 red chilli, de-seeded and finely chopped

1tbsp soy sauce

½tsp each of paprika, ground coriander, and salt

½tbsp lemon juice

1tbsp vegetable oil

Half a 400ml tin of coconut milk

2 skinless chicken breasts, diced

1tbsp chopped fresh coriander

1 Put all the ingredients except the chicken breast, coconut milk and fresh coriander into a blender and blend until smooth.

2 Pour into a heated wok, bring to the boil and cook, stirring continuously, for 2 minutes.

3 Add the coconut milk and chicken breasts and simmer for 10-15 minutes or until the chicken is done and the sauce has thickened. Sprinkle over the fresh coriander and serve.

Janine Lishman-Peat
Thurlstone, South Yorkshire

Family meals are an important part of life in our house, but on Saturday nights my husband and I like to have dinner on our own after the children have eaten. I enjoy cooking something special and rarely do the same thing twice. I'm used to producing a wide range of dishes – my daughter is a vegetarian, while my son doesn't like vegetables at all!

chocolate pots

Rich and smooth, Jonathan Moore's recipe is chocolate heaven and will tempt anyone with a sweet tooth. This recipes makes enough for six, so give the kids a treat before you send them off to bed for the evening!

 Preparing: 5 mins

 Cooking: 5 mins

 Serves 6

 Gluten free

Ingredients

300ml/10fl oz double cream

120g bar of plain chocolate, broken into small pieces, grated or whizzed in a food processor

55g/2oz unsalted butter, cubed

1 Heat the cream in a saucepan until it just begins to bubble, then remove it from the heat.

2 Stir in the chocolate and butter and keep stirring until they have melted. Divide the mixture between 6 small espresso cups. Put the cups on a tray and chill in the refrigerator for a couple of hours.

chef's secret...
Jonathan Moore
Asda development chef

This is a versatile recipe as it can be used unset as a hot chocolate sauce for ice cream, or like a chocolate fondue for dipping fruit. Try adding a little of your favourite liqueur – Tia Maria, Bailey's or Grand Marnier all work well.

choc tips

Melting the chocolate in the hot cream means there's no chance of it burning. Never attempt to melt it in a saucepan over direct heat. You can melt it in the microwave if you have one. Do it for short bursts – just a few seconds – stirring in between each burst.

family fillers

It's bad enough trying to pay the bills at the end of the month without having to think of what to give the kids every night. This chapter is stuffed full of imaginative new dishes as well as more traditional recipes, and they're all fantastic value. So while you're discovering some new family favourites, you'll also be saving money. On top of that, Asda chef Jonathan Moore reveals how he whips up a dessert for his own family in seconds.

hearty bean soup

Good value and welcoming on a cold winter's day, this is a filling and hearty soup – a meal in itself. It actually gets better on standing, so if you don't eat it all in one sitting, it'll be even more delicious the next day!

 Preparing: 10 mins

 Cooking: 1 hour

 Serves 6-8

 Milk and gluten free

Ingredients

115ml/4fl oz olive oil

1 small onion, roughly chopped

3 small sticks of celery, roughly chopped

4 rashers of smoked bacon, chopped

400g can of chopped tomatoes

1tbsp tomato purée

2 chicken stock cubes

2 x 300g cans of cannellini beans

2 x 300g cans of black-eyed beans

Salt and freshly ground black pepper

Fresh basil leaves, to garnish

1 Heat the oil in a large frying pan and gently fry the onions and celery until soft, this should take about 15 minutes.

2 Add the bacon, fry for two minutes, then add the tomatoes and tomato purée and stir in the crumbled stock cubes. Pour in 1 litre/35fl oz of water and simmer on a low heat for 30 minutes.

3 Add the drained beans and simmer for a further 10-15 minutes. Season lightly as the bacon is already salty. Remove from the heat and serve with warm crusty bread. Garnish with a few fresh basil leaves.

the asda chefs say...
To give this soup a real kick, 2 or 3 large, crushed cloves of garlic and ½tsp of crushed chillies.

Andrea Taylor
Hinstock, Shropshire

I grew up in Cyprus and this dish was a family favourite. It's very cheap and very welcoming. I think we usually had it on Wednesdays and there was always plenty left over for the next day.
I started cooking with my mum when I was about 8 or 9 years old and this was one of the first dishes I can remember making. In Greek, it's called fasolada – it's more a stew than a soup, a bit like baked beans!
I thought it would be rather too plain and boring to win a recipe competition, but all my friends told me I should enter it because it's so tasty. I love it because it reminds me of my childhood.

classic italian lasagne

Often the old ones are the best, as this tried and trusted version of lasagne proves. Delicious and good value, it can be made in advance and frozen

 Preparing: 30 mins

 Cooking: 3 hours

 Serves 8

 Long slow cooking

Ingredients

4 x 400g cans of chopped tomatoes

142g tube of tomato purée

2tsp each of Italian seasoning, garlic powder, onion powder, oregano

Spray oil

2 large onions, roughly chopped

1 red pepper and 1 green pepper, de-seeded and chopped

340g/12oz pepperoni, roughly chopped

4 garlic cloves, crushed

1kg/2lb 4oz beef mince

1 egg

375g pack of lasagne

125g pack of mozzarella cheese, sliced

65g/2½oz Parmesan cheese, grated

Salt and freshly ground black pepper

1 Put the tomatoes and tomato purée in a large saucepan and add the seasonings and oregano. Mix well and heat gently. Preheat the oven to 190C/375F/Gas 5.

2 Meanwhile, spray a little oil into a frying pan and cook the onions and peppers until softened. Add to the tomato with the pepperoni and garlic.

3 Mix the mince and egg, and season well. Brown the mince in a non-stick frying pan then add it to the tomato sauce. Cover and simmer for about 2 hours on a low heat. If it becomes too thick, add a little water.

4 Spoon a third of the sauce into an ovenproof dish and cover with a layer of lasagne sheets. Add a third of the mozzarella slices and a sprinkling of Parmesan. Repeat the layers twice more, finishing with the mozzarella and Parmesan cheese.

5 Cover with foil and bake for 15 minutes, then remove the foil and continue to bake for another 45 minutes until brown. Garnish with fresh basil leaves.

the asda chefs say...

Add a glass of red wine to the sauce as it cooks – it will help to create a really rich dish.

Sandra Sullivan
Higher Blackley, Manchester

I come from an Italian background and can still remember, as a little girl, watching my grandma and mum making ravioli and other pasta. I have their recipe for homemade lasagne that's been handed down the generations. Now I'm carrying on the tradition and have passed it to my own daughter too. The version given here requires less preparation. To make lasagne Grandma's way, roll the mince mixture into little balls, brown and simmer in the tomato sauce for about 2 hours. Then remove from the sauce, squash with a potato masher and use to layer up the lasagne.

kate's pasta sauce

If you need help getting your kids to eat vegetables, try this recipe – it's tasty and great value, too

 Preparing: 10 mins

 Cooking: 40 mins

 Serves 4

 Milk and gluten free (Sauce only)

Ingredients

455g/1lb pork mince

1 onion, quartered

2 garlic cloves

1 carrot

1 stick of celery

2 x 400g cans of chopped tomatoes

2tbsp tomato purée

2 green peppers, de-seeded and sliced

1tsp dried oregano

Salt and freshly ground black pepper

1 Gently fry the pork in a non-stick pan until it begins to brown. Pour off any excess fat.

2 Finely chop the onion, garlic, carrot and celery in a food processor.

3 Add the chopped vegetables to the pork and fry for a further 10 minutes, stirring regularly.

4 Add the tomatoes, tomato purée, oregano, peppers and seasoning. Simmer for 20-30 minutes. Serve with spaghetti, or whatever pasta you prefer, and grated cheese.

Ruth Goodwin
Exeter, Devon

This dish was devised by a desperate mum – me! Getting my children to eat healthily can be a battle, but they love tucking into this. As well as containing a selection of nutritious fresh vegetables, the pasta it's served with provides plenty of energy. I'm sure this dish helped my daughter Kate with her gymnastics – she won a medal in her very first competition!

pasta florentino

Packet sauce mixes are great standbys – quick, easy and tasty, they can make a pasta dish really special

Ingredients

500g pack fresh pasta spirals or shells

1 vegetable stock cube

2 x 56g packs savoury white sauce mix

1tbsp finely chopped fresh parsley, plus extra for garnishing

4 eggs

250g bag of baby spinach

3oz/85g dried breadcrumbs

55g/2oz Parmesan cheese, grated

1tsp freshly grated nutmeg

1 Preheat the oven to 200C/400F/ Gas 6. Cook the pasta according to pack instructions and drain.

2 Crumble the stock cube into a jug with the white sauce mix. Add 600ml/1pint boiling water. Add the parsley and season.

3 Crack the eggs into a greased ovenproof dish and cover with the spinach. Mix the pasta with the sauce and add to the dish.

4 Sprinkle the breadcrumbs, cheese and nutmeg over the top. Bake for 20 minutes until golden and garnish with the extra parsley.

Helen Gavito
Perth, Scotland

I make this recipe for myself and my daughter because it's quick, easy and hasn't got too many calories. It's great for when people pop round unexpectedly as the main ingredients are basic store-cupboard foods. I was lucky enough to travel the world as a professional ballet dancer, and I have a passion for Italy – the language, culture and cuisine – so that was probably the inspiration for it!

lamb and red cabbage pasta bake

A healthy variation of a basic lasagne that uses plenty of fresh vegetables. Simple to prepare, filling and good value, too, it's a dish all the family will enjoy

 Preparing: 30 mins

 Cooking: 1 hr 15 mins

 Serves 6

 Freeze uncooked

Ingredients

¼ red cabbage, chopped

1 onion, chopped

2 shallots, peeled and sliced

2tbsp red wine

1dsp each of blackcurrant cordial and apple juice

2tsp olive oil

455g/1lb lamb mince

3 carrots, peeled and chopped

3 sticks of celery, sliced

1 green pepper, de-seeded and chopped

1 lamb stock cube

2 x 400g cans of chopped tomatoes

400g can of kidney beans

2-3tsp mint sauce

1tbsp tomato purée

375g packet of lasagne

2 x 320g jars Asda lasagne and four cheese sauce

55g/2oz Cheddar cheese, grated

1 In a large saucepan, gently simmer the red cabbage in 100ml of water along with the onions, shallots, red wine, cordial and apple juice. Cook gently until the cabbage is softened but still slightly crunchy – this should take about 8-10 minutes. Preheat the oven to 200C/400/F/Gas 6.

2 Heat 1tsp of oil in a large pan, add the lamb and cook until brown. Pour away any fat, then add the carrots, celery and pepper.

3 Crumble in the stock cube and stir in the red cabbage mix, tomatoes, drained kidney beans, mint sauce and the tomato purée. Simmer uncovered on a low heat for 25 minutes to reduce.

4 Lightly grease a deep ovenproof dish with the remaining oil. Make layers of the meat mixture lasagne and cheese sauce, repeating until all the ingredients have been used and ending with a layer of cheese sauce. Sprinkle over the grated cheese. Bake for 30-35 minutes.

the asda chefs say...

If you're not keen on cabbage, this recipe works equally well with leeks. You can also substitute sweet potato for the carrots.

Carol Wilford
Derby, Derbyshire

This is a recipe I devised myself, something I really enjoy doing. In fact, I have hundreds of recipes at home that I've cut from magazines but never bothered to make. I much prefer to play around with different ingredients and come up with something of my own. Then, if my recipe works, I quickly make a note of what I put in it! I had a lot of red cabbage left over from a vegetarian dish I'd made, so I used it to create this 'lasagne with a difference'. It's a good supper dish and you don't even need a side salad. You can freeze it, uncooked, which is very handy, too.

lentil lasagne

A tasty twist on the classic lasagne, this lentil version will feed your family without breaking the bank

 Preparing: 15 mins

 Cooking: 1 hr 15 mins

 Serves 6

 Healthy family meal

Ingredients

1tbsp sunflower oil

455g/1lb beef mince

150g/5½ oz red lentils

1 square of Asda frozen crushed garlic

1 beef stock cube

500g jar of original Bolognese sauce

1 green pepper, de-seeded and diced

375g pack of lasagne

560g jar of lasagne topper

160g pack of mature Cheddar slices

Freshly ground black pepper

1 Preheat the oven to 180C/350F/ Gas 4. Heat the oil in a frying pan and brown the mince. Add the lentils, garlic, Bolognese sauce and seasoning. Crumble in the stock cube and pour in 400ml/ 14fl oz water. Add the green pepper and simmer for 30 mins.

2 In a large ovenproof dish, layer the lasagne sheets alternately with the Bolognese mix, ending with lasagne. Spread lasagne topper over the last layer, then add the cheese. Bake for 30-40 minutes until golden.

Jill Hinnrichs
Dundee, Scotland

I love home-made lasagne, but it can be fiddly to make from scratch. With the help of a few shortcuts from Asda, my recipe still gives you a lovely home-cooked taste. Adding in the lentils gives some added fibre – good for your health! You can also make a tasty vegetarian option by swapping minced beef with frozen minced Quorn or dried veggie mince – you can get both at Asda.

Preparation: 10 mins

 Cooking: 1hr 10 mins

 Serves 6

 Milk and gluten free

Ingredients

680g/1½ lbs beef mince

2tbsp olive oil

1 large onion, finely chopped

340g/12oz button mushrooms, roughly chopped

3 x 215g cans of baked beans

2 x 400g cans of chopped tomatoes

290g can of kidney beans

1tsp paprika

1tsp cayenne pepper

Salt and freshly ground black pepper

1 Brown the mince in a large, non-stick frying pan.

2 Remove the mince from the pan, draining any fat, then add the oil and onions to the pan and gently fry until softened but not browned. Add the mushrooms and cook until soft.

3 Add the mince, baked beans, tomatoes and kidney beans. Stir in the paprika and cayenne pepper and simmer for 45 minutes. Season and serve with rice or baked potatoes.

baked bean chilli

This tasty tummy-filler is a breeze to make, good value and a great standby for wintry nights

Marie Brown
Asda Colleague, Metro Centre

This recipe was given to me about 17 years ago by my sister and I'm still making it – it's perfect for family meals. I wouldn't say I was a fantastic cook, but I love baking, especially cakes. My chocolate cake always goes down well whenever I bring it into work. Working at Asda gives me lots of ideas for things – I often see ingredients in the store and think, "I'll use that in my recipes".

turkey tetrazzini

Waste not, want not – this simple pasta recipe is the perfect solution to those 'what to do with the leftover turkey' dilemmas. Satisfying, nutritious and ideal for anyone who's on a tight budget

 Preparing: 10 mins

 Cooking: 40-50 mins

 Serves 6

 Great value meal

Ingredients

2tbsp olive oil

2 x 454g packs of turkey breast, diced (or use leftover cooked turkey)

500g pack of spaghetti

2 x 15g packs of fresh chives, chopped

2 x 410g cans of cream of mushroom or chicken soup, or a can of each

1 chicken stock cube

55g/2oz Parmesan cheese, finely grated

Freshly ground black pepper

1 If using raw turkey breast, heat the oil and cook the turkey until golden brown, then set aside. Preheat the oven to 190C/375F/Gas 5.

2 Cook the spaghetti for half the amount of time stated in the pack instructions.

3 Reserve 1tbsp of the chives for garnishing. In a bowl, mix the rest of the chives with the cans of soup.

4 Put a quarter of the spaghetti in an ovenproof dish. Spoon a quarter of the soup mix over, then a quarter of the turkey. Continue layering in this way until all the ingredients are used. Season well.

5 Crumble the stock cube in 250ml/9fl oz boiling water and pour over the whole dish. Sprinkle with cheese and bake for 35-45 minutes until the top is golden brown. Garnish with the reserved chives.

the asda chefs say...

Sprinkle a bag of baby spinach leaves between the layers. You can also use chicken, instead of turkey, if you prefer.

Wenda Dyer
Stoke-on-Trent, Staffordshire

This recipe played a part in my most unusual kitchen experience. We used to take part in Renaissance fairs, where people would recreate scenes from history. My husband had made a life-size model of Oliver Cromwell's head to use in the re-enactments and had put it in the oven so the glue he had used would dry. I didn't know this and turned the oven up to pre-heat it. When I went to put the Turkey Tetrazzini in, I was greeted by the sight of the head – its acrylic wig and eyelashes had melted and I was so shocked I nearly dropped the whole lot on the floor!

curry in a hurry

You might think making a curry from scratch takes ages. But this recipe is not only simple and quick to make, it's also great value – working out at about half the cost of a ready-made takeaway meal

 Preparing: 10 mins

 Cooking: 15 mins

 Serves 4

 Milk and gluten free

Ingredients

1 chicken stock cube

2tbsp cornflour

1tbsp vegetable oil

4 skinless chicken breasts, each one cut into 8 pieces

1 onion, roughly chopped

2cm/1in piece root ginger, grated

4 garlic cloves, crushed

2 green chillies, de-seeded and finely sliced (optional)

2tbsp curry powder

1tbsp dark soy sauce

1tbsp tomato ketchup

Salt and freshly ground black pepper

1 Crumble and dissolve the stock cube in 100ml/3½fl oz boiling water, then top up to 600ml/1pint with cold water and leave to cool. Once cooled, blend in the cornflour.

2 In a large saucepan or wok, heat the oil and stir-fry the chicken for around 3 minutes. Add the onion, ginger, garlic and chillies, if using, and cook for a further 5 minutes.

3 Stir in the curry powder and cook for 30 seconds. Add the stock and cornflour, stir well and reduce the heat. Add the soy sauce and ketchup, bring to the boil and simmer gently for 5 minutes or until the sauce has thickened. Season and serve with plain boiled rice.

the asda chefs say...

Fresh chillies are optional – only add them if you like hot, spicy dishes. Watch out for the heat of the curry powder – different brands can vary quite a bit, so use one you are familiar with!

Peter McGuigan
Stanley, Perth

I've been a chef for about 10 years so I've had a lot of practice in creating recipes. I do a lot of the cooking at home – my wife tends to look after the kids' meals at teatime and then I'll throw something together for the two of us later on. I tend to pull all of my recipes out of my head – like everyone else, I'll have a look in the fridge and the cupboards, and then decide what's the best meal I can make with what's there. Having a chef's background is an advantage – I know from experience how separate ingredients will work together and complement each other to create a great taste.

potato-topped beef

With your meat and potatoes in one dish, this meal is simple to make and saves on the washing-up!

 Preparing: 15 mins

 Cooking: 1 hr 10 mins

 Serves 4

 Gluten free

Ingredients

455g/1lb beef mince

1 onion, finely chopped

1 beef stock cube, crumbled

420g can of baked beans

455g/1lb potatoes, peeled and thinly sliced

30g/1oz butter, melted

30g/1oz Cheddar cheese, grated

Salt and freshly ground black pepper

1 Preheat the oven to 190C/375F/Gas 5. Heat a large, non-stick frying pan and brown the mince. Add the onion and fry for 2 minutes. Pour off any excess fat and transfer the mixture into an ovenproof dish.

2 Add the crumbled stock cube, 3tbsp of water and the baked beans. Season well and stir. Arrange the potato slices over the top to cover thinly. Brush the slices with melted butter.

3 Bake for 55 minutes. Sprinkle over the cheese and return to the oven for a further 5 minutes or so until the cheese is golden.

Lyndsey Bruce
Halifax, West Yorkshire

You know the old joke about 101 ways with mince? Well, this recipe came about because I was trying to find a way of making mince more interesting. It's perfect for when you come in from work on a cold winter's evening because it's not too complicated and really fills you up. Everyone who tries it likes it, and it's a hit with kids – they like the baked beans, I think.

Preparing: 10 mins

 Cooking: 1 hour

 Serves 4

 Great for kids

sausage lasagne

Surprise them with something different – this tasty lasagne uses up those store-cupboard standbys

Ingredients

1tbsp olive oil

1 onion, roughly chopped

455g/1lb sausage meat

2 x 420g cans of baked beans

1tsp dried mixed herbs

1tbsp tomato ketchup

375g pack of lasagne

40g packet of cheese sauce mix

300ml/10fl oz milk

55g/2oz Cheddar cheese, grated

1 Preheat the oven to 200C/400F/ Gas 6. Heat the olive oil and gently cook the onion until soft.

2 Add the sausage meat and brown. Drain off the fat. Stir in the beans, herbs and ketchup, then season with pepper.

3 In a large ovenproof dish, layer the meat mixture and lasagne, finishing with a layer of lasagne.

4 Make up the cheese sauce with the milk and pour over the lasagne. Sprinkle over the cheese and bake for 35-40 minutes.

Susan Thorner
Portland, Dorset

I'm pretty adventurous when it comes to food and cooking. If I've got time, I like to experiment and I've got a vast library of cookbooks for inspiration. But I work during the day so family meals have to be quick and easy. When my kids were growing up they liked pasta but not Bologanese sauce – so this recipe was a good way to combine their favourite foods.

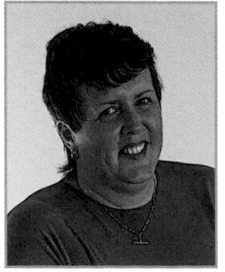

turkey meatballs

These meatballs are baked in a moutwatering tomato sauce – just add pasta and some tasty grated cheese

 Preparing: 20 mins

 Cooking: 50 mins

 Serves 4

 Blender needed

Ingredients

455g/1lb turkey mince

55g/2oz dried breadcrumbs

1 egg

1tbsp vegetable oil

2 onions, finely chopped

4 x 400g cans of chopped tomatoes

6tbsp tomato purée

2 garlic cloves, roughly chopped

2tsp dried oregano

Salt and freshly ground black pepper

1 Preheat the oven to 140C/275F/ Gas 1. Mix together the turkey mince, breadcrumbs, egg and seasoning. Roll into walnut-sized balls with your hands.

2 Heat the oil in a frying pan and brown the meatballs. Remove from the pan and set aside.

3 Gently fry the onion until soft. Smooth the tomatoes, purée and garlic in a blender and pour into an ovenproof dish. Add the meatballs and oregano and bake for 30 minutes. Serve with pasta and grated cheese.

Annamaria Beck

Stoke-on-Trent, Staffordshire

I am British-born, but my parents are Italian and my mum passed down lots of delicious Italian recipes to me. Once a week I cook an Italian meal for my grown-up children, and now my grandchildren love my pasta, too. As we eat Italian at home, when we go out for special occasions we tend to go to a local carvery for some traditional British food!

lou's meatballs

 Preparing: 15 mins

 Cooking: 1 hr 15 mins

 Serves 4-6

 Easy family meal

Parmesan cheese and oregano gives these meatballs real authentic Italian flavour – magnifico!

Ingredients

455g/1lb beef mince

1 egg

100g/3½oz Parmesan cheese, grated

55g/2oz breadcrumbs

1tbsp dried parsley

2½tsp dried oregano

3 garlic cloves, crushed

1tbsp olive oil

2 x 400g cans of chopped tomatoes

100g/3½oz tomato purée

1 bay leaf

1 Mix the mince, egg, Parmesan, breadcrumbs, parsley, 2tsp of the oregano, 2 garlic cloves and seasoning, and form into small balls. Heat the oil in a frying pan and brown the meatballs. Remove from the pan and set aside.

2 Gently fry the rest of the garlic for 1 minute. Add the tomatoes, tomato purée, bay leaf and the rest of the oregano. Simmer for 10 minutes.

3 Return the meatballs to the pan and simmer for 1 hour, stirring frequently. Serve with spaghetti.

Bruce Fraser
Widdrington Station, Northumberland

I reckon these are the best-tasting meatballs you'll ever eat! This recipe is well travelled. It's been passed down from Italy to the United States and now it's come over here to the UK. I just mush all the ingredients together with my hands – that's the Italian way. If you find the tomato sauce a bit too sharp for your taste, simply add a pinch of sugar to it.

herby yorkshires

Golden, crispy and meltingly light, these are the perfect partners for traditional roasts

 Preparing: 25 mins

 Cooking: 25 mins

 Makes 8 puds

 Can be frozen

Ingredients

4tsp sunflower oil

115g/4oz plain flour

2 large eggs, beaten

300ml/10fl oz milk

1tsp dried mixed herbs

1 onion, finely chopped

115g/4oz fresh white breadcrumbs

Salt and freshly ground black pepper

1 Preheat the oven to 200C/400F Gas 6. Put ½tsp of oil into each section of 2 x 4 Yorkshire pudding tins or large muffin tins, and put in the oven to heat.

2 Sieve the flour into a mixing bowl and add seasoning. Make a well in the flour, add the eggs and pour in the milk gradually, beating well as you go, until you have a smooth batter. Set aside for 15 minutes.

3 Add the herbs, onion and breadcrumbs and mix well.

4 When the oil is hot and begins to smoke, spoon the mixture into the tins and bake for 25 minutes.

Douglas Robinson
Asda Colleague, Horwich

My father-in-law was given this recipe by a Maltese chef while serving in the Royal Navy. The first time I tried it was when I visited their house and they were enjoying them with roast pork. It's been a favourite ever since. My wife puts together most of the meals, but I help out. And we always shop at Asda. I work there and get paid to chat – I work on the door as a greeter!

Preparing: 20 mins

 Cooking: 40 mins

 Serves 4-6

 Main or side dish

potato bake

A different way of serving potatoes – mixed with lashings of cheese and topped with onion and bacon

Ingredients

1kg/2lb 4oz baking potatoes, peeled and cut into cubes

225g/8oz Cheddar cheese, grated

1 packet of fresh chives, snipped

55g/2oz butter

6 slices white bread, made into crumbs

1 white onion, finely chopped

250g pack of unsmoked bacon, fat removed, cut into 1cm/½in squares

1tbsp vegetable oil

2tbsp mayonnaise

1 Preheat the oven to 200C/400F/ Gas 6.

2 Boil the potatoes until soft. Mash with 85g/3oz of the cheese, the chives and the butter, then spoon into a large ovenproof dish. In a separate bowl, mix the rest of the cheese with the breadcrumbs.

3 Fry the onion and bacon in the oil until they start to brown. Take off the heat, add the breadcrumb mix and mayonnaise, then spread over the potato and bake for 25 minutes until golden.

Lesley Airey
Cowling, North Yorkshire

My style of cooking could be described as slap-dash! I'm a bit of a stick-in-the-mud and tend to go for meals I know and like, whereas my husband is much more experimental with food. Having said that, I do like to adapt recipes to make them healthier – mainly for weight reasons! This recipe can be made less calorific by using things like reduced fat mayonnaise, cheese and margarine.

yorkshire pizza

Add your own favourite ingredients to this delicious cross between a Yorkshire pudding and a pizza

 Preparing: 30 mins

 Cooking: 1 hr 20 mins

 Serves 6

 Very versatile

Ingredients

2 x 125g packets of batter mix

2 eggs

1tbsp vegetable oil

1 onion, chopped

115g/4oz button mushrooms, roughly chopped

3 tomatoes, roughly chopped

1 skinless chicken breast, diced

30g/1oz butter

200g/7oz Cheddar cheese, grated

1 Preheat the oven to 200C/400F/ Gas 6. Make the batter with the eggs and leave for 20 minutes.

2 Heat the oil in a frying pan and fry the onion until soft. Add the mushrooms and tomatoes and cook until softened. Remove from the pan. Fry the chicken for 5 minutes until cooked.

3 Line a swiss roll tin with foil. Add the butter and put it in the oven for 3 minutes. Rebeat the batter, stir in the onion mixture, chicken and 170g/6oz of the cheese. Pour into the tin, sprinkle over the rest of the cheese and bake for 1 hour.

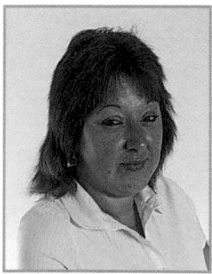

Caron Marsh
West Hull, East Yorkshire

This recipe started as a mistake by my mother-in-law. She was making a Yorkshire pudding one day and accidentally put some onions she was chopping into the mixture. We all thought it was delicious and have been adding different things to it ever since. My children came up with the name – one day they said to me "Mum, why don't you make Yorkshire Pizza?" – and it just stuck.

pig pig pudding

Plenty of onions and herbs make this variation on good old-fashioned toad-in-the-hole really special

Ingredients

300ml/10fl oz semi-skimmed milk

1 large egg

115g/4oz plain flour, sieved

½tsp salt

2 x 454g packs of Cumberland sausages

1 onion, chopped

2tsp dried mixed herbs

1 tbsp lard

1 Preheat the oven to 220C/425F/ Gas 7. Whisk the milk and egg together in a jug. Mix the flour with salt in a bowl. Make a well in the centre. Slowly whisk in the milk mixture until smooth. Leave to stand for 20 minutes.

2 Cook the sausages and onion in a large roasting tin in the oven for about 20 minutes. Drain off the fat, remove from the tin and set aside.

3 Add the herbs to the batter mix. Add the lard to the roasting tin and heat on the hob. Return the sausages and onions to the tin. Pour over the batter and bake for 25-30 minutes until brown.

Tracey Wilkinson

Halifax, West Yorkshire

When I was a kid, my mum always used to make a type of Yorkshire pudding when we had roast pork. She called it seasoning pudding and I've since adapted it to include tasty sausages for a good, winter warmer. The aroma that fills the kitchen while it's cooking is so enticing. My daughter's got a toy pig called 'Pig Pig' – and that's how this dish got its name.

deliciously easy desserts!

Jonathan Moore
Asda innovation chef

'A lot of the time when I'm cooking a meal for my family or friends, I'm so busy thinking about the main course that I don't have time to worry about a pudding. With Asda's great range of ready-made desserts, it's not a problem, but I do like to add my own special touch. Try these ideas.'

1 Ice cream is just about the easiest dessert there is – keep a tub of vanilla ice cream in the freezer and you can't go wrong...
● Fill a brandy snap basket with a large scoop of vanilla ice cream and top with canned peach slices. Pour over some fruit coulis or sauce and serve.
● Letting the kids help make their own desserts is a great way to introduce them to cooking – our son Joshua (right) loves to decorate a couple of scoops of ice cream with chocolate sauce and lots of his favourite sweets.

2 On a cold winter's night, nothing beats a warm pud. There are plenty of old favourites you can rely on, but try adding a little something extra...
● To add a luxurious twist to a hot bread and butter pudding, melt a jar of jam from Asda's Extra Special range in a saucepan, pass it through a sieve, then serve as an accompaniment to the pudding.
● Serve a nice warm jam roly poly with lightly whipped cream that has been flavoured with vanilla extract.

3 With such a huge variety of fruits available all year round, we're spoilt for choice. Here are three ideas for adding a burst of flavour to your dessert.
● To transform a plain cheesecake into something really pretty, serve it with some crushed berries that have been dusted with icing sugar.
● Top a pavlova with raspberries that have been pre-soaked in kirsch or, for an alcohol-free version, soak the fruit in a little orange juice.
● Add some oomph to a fruit salad by warming a little water and sugar until melted. Cool, then add a tot of dark rum and pour over the fruit.

helping hands

It's pretty difficult to keep children out of the kitchen when you're putting together a dessert so why not include them in what you are doing. It doesn't matter how simple it looks, given the opportunity, kids will revel in the chance to make their own puddings. Whether it's helping to make biscuits or simply sprinkling their favourite sweets onto ice cream and jelly, children enjoy getting busy in the kitchen just as much as they enjoy eating the results.

pear clafoutis

This hot fruity pud is incredibly easy to make. A delicious, vanilla-flavoured custardy batter covers sweet, succulent pears. If you have a little extra time on your hands to make a special pud, this one is well worth the effort

 Preparing: 10 mins

 Cooking: 35-40 mins

 Serves 8

 Impressive but easy

Ingredients

30g/1oz butter, softened

455g/1lb ripe pears, peeled, cored and sliced

4 eggs

85g/3oz plain flour

85g/3oz caster sugar, plus 1tbsp to decorate

225ml/8fl oz double cream

225ml/8fl oz milk

2tsp vanilla essence

Pinch of salt

1 Preheat the oven to 200C/400F/Gas 6.

2 Grease a 25cm/10in tart tin or flan dish with the butter. Arrange the pears in a single layer in the base.

3 Whisk all the remaining ingredients together or whizz in a liquidiser until they form a smooth batter.

4 Pour the batter over the pears and bake for 35-40 minutes until the pudding is well-risen, golden and firm. Allow to stand for 5 minutes, sprinkle with the extra caster sugar and serve straightaway.

the asda chefs say...

If you want to add a little spice, mix ½tsp of ground cinnamon into the batter before pouring over the pears. This is delicious served warm, with a generous scoop of vanilla ice cream, or a dollop of crème fraîche.

Sarah Brookfield
Asda Colleague, Leeds

Home economics was always my favourite subject at school and as the new editor of *Asda Magazine*, I'm now lucky enough to have a job that involves food as well! I love baking and I also enjoy entertaining. I try to find recipes that are easy to make but look impressive, too, and this one is a good example – it looks a lot harder to make than it is. My favourite things to make are salads and fish – really simple things that are packed with flavour. My summer fruit muffins have become pretty famous, too!

chocolate meringue pudding

The warm meringue and cool ice cream are an irresistible combination and the chocolate spread makes this a baked Alaska with a difference. One for the sweet toothed!

 Preparing: 25 mins

 Cooking: 30 mins

 Serves 6

 Special family treat

Ingredients

115g/4oz soft margarine, plus 1tsp for greasing

265g/9½oz caster sugar

2 whole eggs, beaten, plus 3 egg whites

75g/2½oz plain chocolate, broken into pieces

115g/4oz self-raising flour

½tsp vinegar

1tsp cornflour

200ml/7fl oz chocolate spread

500ml block of vanilla ice cream

30g/1oz hazelnuts, chopped

1 Preheat the oven to 180C/350F/Gas 4. Grease the base of a 20cm/8in round cake tin, then line it with greaseproof paper or baking parchment.

2 Beat the margarine and 115g/4oz of the caster sugar together until pale in colour and increased in volume. Add the 2 whole eggs, one at a time, beating well after each addition. Fold in the chocolate and flour. Put the mixture into the tin and bake for 25 minutes.

3 Turn the sponge out of the tin onto a wire rack to cool. Turn the oven up to 220C/425F/Gas 7.

4 Make the meringue. In a clean bowl, whisk the 3 egg whites and add the vinegar and cornflour. Continue whisking, gradually adding the remaining caster sugar, until it's all used and the mixture forms stiff peaks.

5 Spread the chocolate mixture onto the cake, put the ice cream on top, then completely cover the cake and ice cream with meringue. Scatter over the hazelnuts and bake for a few minutes until the meringue sets.

the adsa chefs say...

To make perfect meringue, whisk the egg whites in a spotlessly clean, dry bowl. For extra choccie flavour, serve with a drizzle of chocolate sauce (see the chocolate pots recipe on page 101).

Susan Johnson
Goole, East Yorkshire

My mum gave me her recipe for baked Alaska and I've been making it for 30 years. This version has chocolate added, which makes it a bit different. A lot of people can be a bit worried about making meringue, I think because sometimes it can go a bit flat, and I did have a few problems the first couple of times I made it. But I think a lot of cooking is about learning from your mistakes. It took me years before I could make a sponge cake – mine were always terrible and rock hard!

got to
be good

These recipes prove that looking after your health can be absolutely delicious. Most of the dishes are low in saturated fat as well as in calories, but there are still a few treats – the Tuscan Orange Cake shows just how tasty low-fat food can be! The Asda chefs reveal how you can add flavour to dishes without adding calories. And if your friends or family are watching their weight, this chapter will help you serve up meals that will leave them feeling virtuous as well as satisfied.

adding taste without calories

Neil Nugent
Asda innovation chef

"A lot of people think low calorie means no flavour, but there are loads of ways to make food taste great and keep it healthy, too. There are four basic groups of natural flavour-boosters and by combining them, you can create endless taste combinations. Here's how..."

1 Acidity helps bring out the flavour of other ingredients. You can use citrus juice – lemon, lime or orange, or vinegars – rice wine, balsamic, wine or cider vinegars are all perfect.

2 Seasonings also help bring out the natural flavours in other foods. They include sea salt, freshly-ground pepper, sugar, anchovies, soy sauce, Worcestershire sauce and Thai fish sauce.

3 Distinctive aroma-led flavour comes from things such as fragrant spices and herbs including lemongrass, five spice powder, cumin, ground coriander, turmeric and cardamom.

4 Pungency or heat can be added by chilli, horseradish, fresh root ginger, garlic, onions, all types of mustard or pepper derivatives such as paprika and Tabasco.

now try this!

Take at least one flavour from each of the four groups – acidity, seasonings, pungency and aroma-led flavour – and combine them to make a marinade for chicken, fish, meat or vegetables, or use as a sauce or dressing. For a Thai combination, mix 4tbsp rice wine vinegar, 1 finely chopped red chilli, 2tbsp chopped coriander leaf and sugar to taste (add 2tbsp fish sauce too, if you like). For a French-style flavour, mix 4tbsp cider vinegar, 1tsp Dijon mustard, 1tbsp chopped parsley and black pepper to taste. Or for a Chinese-style combination, mix 4tbsp rice wine vinegar, a half-inch piece of chopped fresh root ginger, ½tsp five spice powder and soy sauce.

tomato spaghetti

This dish costs next to nothing and is so tasty, you won't even realise that it's healthy, too. If you're really watching the calories, just leave out the Parmesan cheese – and make sure you don't go back for seconds!

 Preparing: 5 mins

 Cooking: 35 mins

 Serves 4

 **Per serving –
Fat: 13g, Calories: 480**

Ingredients

1tbsp olive oil

2 large onions, finely chopped

2 garlic cloves, crushed

1tsp dried oregano

1tsp dried marjoram

3 x 400g cans of chopped plum tomatoes

2 bay leaves

1tbsp sugar (optional)

1tsp salt (optional)

1 vegetable stock cube

455g/1lb dried spaghetti

85g/3oz Parmesan cheese, grated, or a few rocket leaves, to garnish

Freshly ground black pepper

1 In a large saucepan, heat the oil and gently fry the onion for 10 minutes until soft, then add the garlic and cook for a further minute.

2 Add the oregano and marjoram and then fry gently for another 3 minutes to infuse all the flavours.

3 Add the tomatoes, bay leaves, sugar and salt, if using. Season with black pepper, then crumble in the stock cube and bring to the boil. Simmer for 15-20 minutes stirring occasionally.

4 Meanwhile, cook the spaghetti according to the pack instructions. Serve with the sauce spooned over and the grated cheese or rocket leaves on top.

the asda chefs say...

Pack instructions for cooking pasta are a guide and it's always a good idea to taste a bit so you can tell if it's done to your liking. Some people like it really soft, but these days most people like it with a bit of bite, otherwise known as 'al dente'.

Sara Read
Fareham, Hampshire

This is a recipe with a bit of family tradition. My auntie was Italian and this was her speciality. It wasn't long before my mum picked up the dish – she, in turn, passed it on to me – and I expect my kids will be quizzing me about it before long. Simple to make and ready in under an hour, this low fat classic is a really tasty meal that will satisfy all appetites and leave you with the time to put your feet up and watch your favourite TV shows.

carol's quick pasta

Canned tuna gives this pasta dish plenty of flavour – buy the variety in brine to keep the calories down

 Preparing: 10 mins

 Cooking: 17 mins

 Serves: 2

 **Per serving –
Fat: 6g, Calories: 433
Milk free**

Ingredients

1 large onion, roughly chopped

85g/3oz mushrooms, sliced

4 rashers of back bacon, cut into strips

185g can of tuna chunks in brine

400g can of chopped tomatoes with herbs or garlic

Half a 15g pack of fresh basil or chives, roughly chopped

225g/8oz Quick Cook fusilli

1 Dry fry the onions in a non-stick pan with no oil for 5 minutes. Add the mushrooms and cook for a further 2 minutes.

2 Add the bacon and cook for another 5 minutes. Add the tuna, tomatoes and fresh herbs.

3 Cook the pasta for 5 minutes and continue to cook the sauce for the same amount of time.

4 Drain the pasta and add it to the sauce. Mix well and serve.

the asda chefs say...

Try adding chopped red peppers, celery or sweetcorn to make it more filling.

Carol Rice
Asda Colleague, Wrexham

I made this recipe up to help me with weight loss. And it worked – so much so that I still use it whenever I discover that I've gained a pound or two. It's so versatile, as you can add more to it if you want to serve it as a main meal in the evening, or just make up the basic recipe featured here if you want a light meal. I usually have it for dinner and then take any leftovers to work the next day.

Preparing: 10 mins

 Cooking: 12 mins

 Serves: 4

 **Per serving –
Fat: 1g, Calories: 220
Milk free**

Ingredients

9 dried tagliatelle nests

**2 leeks, washed, cut in half lengthwise
then cut into 1cm/½in pieces**

1 red pepper, de-seeded and sliced

1 yellow pepper, de-seeded and sliced

85g/3oz mange tout, cut in half

150ml/5fl oz white wine

½tsp dried tarragon

1tbsp coarse-grain mustard

1 Cook the pasta according to
the pack instructions and add
the leeks to the pan for the last
five minutes of cooking. Add the
rest of the vegetables for the last
2-3 minutes of cooking.

2 Meanwhile, in a separate pan,
simmer the remaining ingredients
and any seasoning until reduced
by half.

3 Drain the pasta and vegetables,
return to the pan, add the wine
reduction, stir and serve.

the asda chefs say...

If you like spicy food, why not add ½tsp
dried crushed chillies.

vegetable pasta

A healthy vegetarian dish that's bursting with flavour
and colour – without any hidden calories!

**Pennie
Cowley**
Rossendale, Lancashire

I get most of my recipes
from friends and family,
and I love this recipe
because it's quick and
easy. It's also vegetarian
and by my estimation,
comes in at just over 200
calories for each serving.
It uses a bit of wine, so I
usually buy one of the
small 250ml bottles that
Asda sell, which means
there's just enough left
over for me to enjoy a
quick tipple while
I'm cooking!

romerjo salad

This recipe is an unusual salad that uses ingredients you might not otherwise think of combining, but they work brilliantly together. It's also a dish that proves being healthy can be delicious, too!

 Preparing: 20 mins

 Cooking: 10 mins

 Serves 2

 **Per serving –
Fat: 27g, Calories: 420
Gluten free**

Ingredients

100g/3½oz smoked haddock

150ml/5fl oz milk

1 bay leaf

5 whole black peppercorns

1 red onion, sliced

50ml/2fl oz extra virgin olive oil

2 large navel oranges, peeled and segmented

A handful each of fresh spinach and fresh watercress

1 bunch parsley, coarsely chopped

Freshly ground black pepper

1 In a large saucepan, gently poach the haddock in enough milk to cover it, along with the bay leaf and black peppercorns, for 10 minutes. Leave to cool for 5 minutes, then drain and remove the fish from the pan and break it up into large flakes.

2 Put the flaked haddock into a large salad bowl, then add the onion and olive oil. Toss gently and leave for 5-10 minutes.

3 Add the oranges, spinach, watercress and chopped parsley. Season with freshly ground black pepper and serve.

nice and zesty

The sweet navel oranges give this salad a really distinctive zing. It's important to remove all the pith from the orange, as this can give a bitter taste. To segment the orange, just peel it with a sharp knife, then slice down either side of the membrane that separates each segment.

chef's secret...
Neil Nugent
Asda innovation chef

Adding the oil and onion to the fish when it's still slightly warm allows the flavours to develop well. The same thing happens when you're making potato salad – always add the dressing when the potatoes are still warm so they will take up all the flavour of the dressing.

chicken stir-fry

This spicy, Oriential-style stir-fry is quick to make and delicious to eat! If you leave out the chicken altogether for a healthier vegetarian version, you'll save on the pennies as well as the calories!

 Preparing: 35 mins

 Cooking: 15 mins

 Serves 4

 **Per serving –
Fat: 12g, Calories: 270
Milk and gluten free**

Ingredients

For the sauce

1tsp each of light soy sauce and dark soy sauce

2tsp cornflour

1tsp sesame oil

1 chicken stock cube

For the marinade

1tsp mixed peppercorns, ground

2tbsp dark soy sauce

1tsp cornflour

2tsp dry sherry

For the stir-fry

455g/1lb skinless chicken breasts, diced

2tbsp sunflower oil

5 spring onions, chopped

5cm/2in piece root ginger, peeled and chopped

3 garlic cloves, sliced

50g pack of mixed chillies, de-seeded and sliced

3 assorted peppers, de-seeded and sliced

1. For the sauce, mix together the light and dark soy sauces with the cornflour and sesame oil. Crumble the stock cube in 300ml/10fl oz boiling water and stir in the soy sauce mixture. Set aside.

2. Mix all the marinade ingredients together, add the chicken and leave to marinate for at least 15 minutes. Drain the chicken and discard the liquid.

3. Heat 1tbsp of the oil in a large frying pan, and stir-fry the spring onions for 5 minutes until just brown. Remove from the pan and set aside.

4. Add the remaining oil to the pan and stir-fry the chicken for 3-4 minutes. Add the ginger, garlic, chillies and peppers and stir-fry for a further 2 minutes.

5. Add the spring onion and the sauce mixture, reduce the heat and cook for 3-4 minutes until the sauce thickens. Serve with egg noodles or rice.

the asda chefs say...

Try adding some beansprouts, sesame seeds and carrots cut into matchsticks. You can use lean pork instead of chicken.

Stephen Leatherbarrow
Oldham, Greater Manchester

This stir-fry is the kind of food we eat all the time in our family. A lot of our meals tend to be Indian, Mexican or Thai in origin, I suppose. Having said that, we often go to book fairs and buy really old cookery books for about 50p or £1, and they're so interesting – full of traditional English food – the kind of thing I grew up watching my mum make. This meal is quick to cook, but the preparation takes a bit of time. In a funny way, I find that to be the best part. I just crack open a bottle of wine and get on with the chopping.

chicken with ham

Using skinless chicken breasts keeps this recipe healthy, wrapping them in ham keeps them moist

 Preparing: 5 mins

 Cooking: 35 mins

 Serves: 4

 Per serving –
Fat: 5g, Calories: 240
Milk and gluten free

Ingredients

4 skinless chicken breasts

200g/7oz wafer thin ham

250g pack of button mushrooms, cut in half

115ml/4fl oz white wine (optional)

330ml can of ginger ale

Salt and freshly ground black pepper

1 Preheat the oven to 190C/375F Gas 5.

2 Wrap each piece of chicken in ham. Place in an ovenproof dish with a lid.

3 Add the mushrooms, wine and enough ginger ale to cover the chicken. Season well, cover and bake in the oven for 30 minutes.

4 Remove the chicken, reduce the sauce for 5 minutes and season well.

the asda chefs say...

Add 2tbsp chopped parsley before serving. For a more special version, use slices of Parma ham, instead of wafer thin ham.

Rosemary Piddington
Horsforth, West Yorkshire

I usually cook a meal from scratch every night, and this is my favourite. My mum first cooked it for me as a treat, and it's really delicious served with mashed potatoes with fromage frais, some lemon juice squeezed over and lots of green vegetables on the side. Use tinned mushrooms for convenience and, if you're feeling indulgent, add a splash of single cream to the sauce.

Preparing: 20 mins

 Cooking: 5-6 mins

 Serves: 4

 **Per serving –
Fat: 5g, Calories: 185
Milk and gluten free**

Ingredients

455g/1lb chicken goujons

1tsp olive oil

3 lemons, halved

3 garlic cloves, crushed

1 red onion, finely chopped

2½cm/1in piece of root ginger,
finely chopped

2 red or green chillies, de-seeded and
finely chopped, or 1tsp dried crushed
red chillies

4 vine-ripened tomatoes, chopped

200g pack of iceberg lettuce, shredded

1½tbsp fish sauce or ½tsp salt

Freshly ground black pepper

1 Fry the chicken in the oil for
5-6 minutes until cooked. Allow
to cool, then tear into bite-sized
pieces. Squeeze over the juice
of half a lemon.

2 Put the garlic, onion, ginger,
chillies, tomatoes, lettuce and
chicken in a bowl. Pour over
the fish sauce and mix well.

3 Squeeze the remaining lemon
halves over the whole salad.
Season with pepper and serve.

spicy chicken salad

If you like chicken salad, this one is a spicy surprise!
As well as being tasty, it's good value and healthy

Richard Downs

Asda Colleague, Hull Bilton

I love this recipe because
all the ingredients are
healthy and very good
for you. It is also cheap,
and for those who think
it's just a chicken salad,
they're in for a spicy
surprise. I have my
mother to thank for my
love of cooking and see
it more as a hobby rather
than a daily chore. When
I'm at home I indulge
myself in the kitchen with
as many exotic spices as I
can lay my hands on!

lemon pepper chicken

This tasty tagliatelle and chicken dish can be made in a flash and it's full of flavour, without too many calories. It'll add a splash of colour to your table, too!

 Preparing: 5 mins

 Cooking: 15 mins

 Serves: 4

 **Per serving –
Fat: 12g, Calories: 385
Milk free**

Ingredients

2tbsp olive oil

2 skinless chicken breasts, cut into thin strips across the breast

400g can of tomatoes

2tsp lemon pepper seasoning

310g pack of broccoli, cut into bite-sized florets

2 x 300g packs of fresh tagliatelle

Freshly ground black pepper

1 Put a large pan of water on to boil for the pasta.

2 Heat the oil in a large frying pan over a moderate heat, add the chicken and stir-fry for 5-6 minutes until brown.

3 Add the tomatoes and the lemon pepper and continue to cook for a further 10 minutes to thicken the sauce.

4 Put the broccoli and pasta into the boiling water and cook for 3 minutes. Drain well and season. Serve the chicken on top of the tagliatelle and broccoli.

Matt McGlashan
Bolton, Lancashire

This is a favourite dish of mine. It's really quick and works just as well as a meal for friends as it does served as a simple tea for a hungry family. I just made it up one day when I wanted to cook something with more to it than just pasta and veg. I enjoy making things up as I go along. Sometimes I'll use a cook book, but more often than not I adapt recipes to suit what I've got in the fridge.

the asda chefs say...

If you prefer a fresh lemon taste, instead of the lemon pepper seasoning add ½tsp salt, ½tsp ground black pepper and the grated zest and juice of a lemon.

crispy lemon haddock

A crispy, lemony coating makes this haddock really special – and with no frying it's deliciously healthy. Serve with lots of fresh vegetables to make it even better

 Preparing: 20 mins

 Cooking: 15-20 mins

 Serves: 4

 Per serving –
Fat: 15, Calories: 200
Milk free

Ingredients

4tbsp sunflower oil

2tbsp red wine vinegar

Juice of half a lemon

115g/4oz fresh breadcrumbs

4 skinless haddock fillets

Salt and freshly ground black pepper

1 Preheat the oven to 200C/400F/Gas 6.

2 Mix the oil, vinegar, lemon juice and seasoning in a shallow dish. Put the breadcrumbs in another shallow dish and season well.

3 Dry the fish with kitchen paper and dip it in the oil and vinegar mixture, then coat with breadcrumbs on both sides.

4 Put the fish on a non-stick baking sheet. Drizzle with any of the remaining oil and vinegar mix and leave for 10 minutes.

5 Bake for 15-20 minutes, turning halfway through. Serve with new potatoes, carrots and courgettes, or a green salad.

Mike Johnson
Holburn, Aberdeen

My dad used to make this all the time. It's quick, easy and healthy, too – he was on a low-fat diet at the time. I used to be a chef at a hotel in Inverness, so I like to invent new things and I'm always looking in books, magazines and on TV for inspiration. What's my worst ever cooking disaster? I once got the sugar and salt shakers mixed up and put sugar on 200 rounds of sandwiches!

the asda chefs say...

Try using lime instead of lemon and add some chopped mixed nuts to the breadcrumbs for a crunchier texture.

tasty bean mince

Here's a great winter warmer that's really nutritious – the beans make the mince go a lot further, so it's good value, too. If you like, you can leave out the meat altogether to make it lower in fat and suitable for vegetarians

 Preparing: 10 mins

 Cooking: 1 hr 20 mins

 Serves 4

 **Per serving –
Fat: 11g, Calories: 285
Milk free**

Ingredients

225g/8oz lean minced beef

½tbsp vegetable oil

1 large onion, roughly chopped

2 garlic cloves, crushed

2 beef stock cubes

1 red pepper, de-seeded and sliced

1 green pepper, de-seeded and sliced

170g/6oz button mushrooms, sliced

400g can of red kidney beans

400g can of whole tomatoes

400g can of baked beans

Freshly ground black pepper

1 Preheat the oven to 180C/350F/Gas 4.

2 Brown the mince in a non-stick frying pan for 10 minutes, or cook in the microwave for 5 minutes on HIGH. Drain off any fat and set aside.

3 Heat the oil in the pan and gently fry the onion for 15-20 minutes until soft. Return the mince to the pan and add the garlic. Crumble the stock cubes in 600ml/1pint of boiling water and add it to the pan.

4 Add the peppers, mushrooms, kidney beans, tomatoes and baked beans. Cook on a high heat for 10 minutes. Transfer to a large ovenproof dish and season with black pepper.

5 Bake for 40 minutes, stirring 2 or 3 times. Serve with lightly cooked broccoli and baked potatoes.

the asda chefs say...

For a vegetarian version, omit the mince and add more canned beans – try borlotti and black-eyed beans for a change.

Kath Wilson
Harrogate, North Yorkshire

This recipe is my emergency concoction for unexpected guests – it's cheap, tasty and healthy. I don't actually have a favourite food, but I always enjoy using good quality raw ingredients. We don't really eat convenience foods – I love to cook, and so I make sure that we have a fresh, home-cooked meal every day. I enjoy watching Ainsley Harriott on the television because he has such a relaxed approach to cooking. I believe that cooking isn't a chore, but a real pleasure, and Ainsley always gets this across with his humour and flamboyant style!

sunshine fruit cake

For a really healthy teatime treat this flavoursome fruit cake is hard to beat. Use your favourite combination of dried fruits from Asda's Extra Special range and watch your guests come back for seconds and thirds!

 Preparing: 35 mins

 Cooking: 45 mins

 Makes 12 slices

 **Per slice –
Fat: 3g, Calories: 180**

Ingredients

1 Earl Grey tea bag

250g pack of Extra Special Taste of Florida fruit

15g/½oz softened butter

225g/8oz self-raising flour, sieved

55g/2oz dark brown sugar

1tbsp thick-cut marmalade

1 egg, beaten

30g/1oz chopped nuts

½tsp mixed spice

1 Put the tea bag into 150ml/5fl oz of boiling water, leave for 3 minutes then remove and pour the tea over the dried fruit. Leave to soak for 30 minutes.

2 Preheat the oven to 180C/350F/Gas 4. Grease a 1.2 litre/2 pint loaf tin with the butter.

3 Mix the fruit and its liquid with all the other ingredients – if it seems a bit dry, add a little milk. Spoon the mixture into the loaf tin and cook in the middle of the oven for about 45 minutes. Test with a skewer to see if it's cooked – if it comes out clean, it's done; if not, cook for a few minutes more.

4 Cool on a wire rack before slicing and serving. This will keep for 2-3 days in an airtight container.

Dreena Booth
Hinckley, Leicestershire

I've always tried to cook healthily for me and my family, although of course we do have the occasional naughty thing like fish and chips as a treat! My husband and I share the cooking in our household, although he probably likes to cook more than I do. We have tried to pass on our enthusiasm to our grown-up sons, and my youngest now cooks for his family every day. I like to eat more traditional English dishes, but I do also fancy the occasional pasta dish or pizza. I've been on holiday to Italy in the past and really fell in love with the food.

the asda chefs say...

You can use any mixture of dried fruit you happen to have in your cupboard. To save time, microwave the fruit and tea on HIGH for 3 minutes and you won't need to let it soak.

tuscan orange cake

This recipe makes one cake and 12 muffins – if by some chance you don't eat them all, pop them in the freezer for another time! Low in fat, but high in taste, the oranges give it a rich, zesty flavour

 Preparing: 1 hour

 Cooking: cake, 40 mins; muffins, 15-20 mins

 Makes 1 cake (10 slices) and 12 muffins

 Per muffin – Fat: 8.5g, Calories: 150

Ingredients

2 oranges

15g/½oz butter, softened

9 eggs

340g/12oz caster sugar

25g/1oz plain flour

340g/12oz ground almonds

1½tsp baking powder

1 Boil the oranges gently for an hour until soft. Cut in half, remove any pips then blitz the oranges, including the skin, in a food processor until it's a chunky purée.

2 Preheat the oven to 180C/350C/Gas 4. Grease a 25cm/10in round springform cake tin with the butter and line the base with greaseproof paper. Put paper muffin cases in the muffin tin.

3 Whisk the eggs and sugar together in a large bowl until thick. Sift in the flour, then fold in the almonds and baking powder. Fold in the orange purée.

4 Pour the mixture into the cake tin and muffin cases. Bake the cake for 40 minutes and the muffins for the final 15-20 minutes. Cover the top of the cake with greaseproof paper if it gets too brown.

5 Cool for 15 minutes before turning out. Serve with Greek yogurt flavoured with orange liqueur and orange segments.

chef's secret...
Jonathan Moore
Asda innovation chef

To make an even more citrussy cake, substitute one of the oranges for a lemon. This recipe freezes really well.

low-fat cakes

Most people think of cakes and they think of calories and fat, but it is possible to create delicious cakes that are low in fat. The butter or margarine used in most cakes helps to keep them moist, so if you leave that out, you need something to replace it. In this recipe, it's the oranges that do the job, but you can also use other fruits, such as apples or dried fruits, and grated carrots. I've even tried a cake that uses grated courgettes. Try a few variations and see what you can come up with...